"Cooper Lawrence manages to combin realities beautifully in this page-turn read!"

—Jai Rodriguez, *Queer Eye for the Straight Guy*

"Dating can be a painful experience; it's nice to throw a little humor on the subject."

—Rachel Perry, host, *VH1: All Access*

"*Been There, Done That, Kept the Jewelry* is the smartest dating book I've read in years. Every woman who reads it will recognize at least one guy she's dated in the list of types—but these aren't the usual cliche types; these are true, real-life ones that we all rationalize away as we date them, hearts full of hope, only to face the crushing truth after we've wasted too much time. The idea that with each failed relationship there is a lesson you MUST learn, so you can avoid heading down the same road, is the only way a modern woman can date. I always say 'there's no such thing as a bad date—only good dates, and funny stories!' And this book is filled with bittersweet—yet still often funny—stories of failed romance that any reader can learn from without having to go through it herself. This book is like all of your girlfriends getting together to tell dating war stories . . . and from those stories you can create your personal, unofficial 'strategy' for finding the relationship you're looking for. Best of all, it leaves even the most jaded (borderline bitter!) dater with that glimmer of, 'Well, maybe I can give this one more try . . . .'"

—Susan Schulz, Editor-in-Chief, *CosmoGirl*

been there, done that,
Kept the Jewelry

Find True Love—Turn Your Tarnished Dating
Past into a Brilliant Romantic Future

Cooper Lawrence

POLKA DOT PRESS
Avon, Massachusetts

Published by
Polka Dot Press, an imprint of Adams Media,
an F+W Publications Company
57 Littlefield Street
Avon, MA 02322
www.adamsmedia.com

ISBN 10: 1-59337-635-9
ISBN 13: 978-1-59337-635-2

Printed in the United States of America.

J I H G F E D C B A

Library of Congress Cataloging-in-Publication Data
Lawrence, Cooper.
Been there, done that, kept the jewelry / by Cooper Lawrence.
p.   cm.
Includes bibliographical references and index.
ISBN 1-59337-635-9
1. Dating (Social customs) 2. Man-woman relationships. I. Title.
HQ801.L337 2006
646.7'7082—dc22
2006013684

This publication is designed to provide accurate and authoritative information with regard
to the subject matter covered. It is sold with the understanding that the publisher is not
engaged in rendering legal, accounting, or other professional advice. If legal advice or other
expert assistance is required, the services of a competent professional person should be
sought.
—From a *Declaration of Principles* jointly adopted by a Committee of the
American Bar Association and a Committee of Publishers and Associations

Many of the designations used by manufacturers and sellers to distinguish their product are
claimed as trademarks. Where those designations appear in this book and Adams Media
was aware of a trademark claim, the designations have been printed with initial capital
letters.

Author Photo: Bill Ray; *Hair by:* James Corbett; *Cut by:* Andre Tartavernise;
Styling by: Ronin Fleischman; *Makeup by:* Stephanie Barr

Interior illustrations by: Steve Heimann

This book is available at quantity discounts for bulk purchases.
For information, please call 1-800-872-5627.

contents

acknowledgments

First, I must thank all the women who participated in my research, especially those who selflessly divulged all of their dating experiences—the good, the bad, and the "you'll never believe this one." None of this would have been possible, however, without my wonderful agent and friend, Maura Teitelbaum, who believed in me right from the very beginning, and who helped celebrate my keeping the jewelry by dancing all night long at my wedding. Which brings me to my most precious find, my husband, Sean Lee, living proof that there is someone special out there for everyone. Without his humor, support, and patience, I wouldn't know what it was like to be truly loved, nor would I have believed my own advice! That said I should take this opportunity to thank all of the *Been There, Done That* guys who led me to where I am now and the lessons I learned from them, like how to spot a jewel, which did not come naturally for me. For example, after one date with a now famous multimillionaire talk show host and comic, I decided that he was going nowhere and didn't want to waste my time, so instead I hooked up with an art director from MTV, who, after two years, ended up living on my couch.

I would also like to thank everyone at Adams Media and Polka Dot Press, especially Gary Krebs, Scott Watrous, Karen Cooper, Beth Gissinger, and Kirsten Amann. Without Kirsten's

viii   *been there, done that, kept the jewelry*

wonderful sense of humor and overall smarty-pants abilities, this book would only be sort of brilliant. I would like to give an individual thank-you to Danielle Chiotti, who shaped this book and expanded the realm of possibilities. Great big love and thanks to my parents, Sandi and Robert Durell, for always being supportive of their "blue-chip investment," and to Jon Lee, who let me steal some of his best jokes, as well as his son.

premarital dating:
the plight of the singlectual

i adore wearing gems, but not because they
are mine. you can't possess radiance, you
can only admire it.

—elizabeth taylor

You don't have to tell me what it's like to still be single after dating for so long; I know, firsthand. I was a single woman for many, many, many years. Actually, many more years than my mother would have preferred. So, while I can empathize as a psychologist, I can also relate as a woman.

You have dated . . . and dated . . . and dated . . . and where the hell is he already, right? You bought the Manolos (or at least the really great knockoffs), went to the dating services, dyed your hair, cut your hair, grew your hair, bedazzled your clothing, flirted, primped, pumped, and exfoliated, and you have seen more blind dates than the maitre d' at Balthazar, so how is it possible that you are still single? It's not that you haven't tried; you have been in relationships . . . many, many relationships. You went on a few vacations, met some parents, and even have some jewelry to show for it! But that one piece of jewelry, the deal-sealing symbol of lifelong commitment, still eludes you. Even if you aren't in this for the ring, you deserve a real relationship. Somehow, though, you keep finding yourself involved with one dating disaster after another. Your love life makes *Sex and the City* look like *Gilmore Girls*, yet somehow no man has been able to tie you down (tie you *up* maybe, but not tie you down). You, my friend, are a Singlectual.

> **Singlectual:** *n* (single-ek´-tual)
> A single woman who is smart and has certainly been there, done that. She has fabulous friendships and even some great love stories to tell, but alas, for some strange twist of fate is still single and doesn't want to be.

Why would that be? That is what *Been There, Done That, Kept the Jewelry* is designed to help you figure out. We will start with an honest look at the most popular breeds of men that the Singlectual has dated, and examine and dissect how your interaction with men in their natural habitats has led you to your current plight: fabulous, highly datable, and unnecessarily single. We will use this knowledge to help you learn how to spot the men to pass on, and how to recognize the one you will keep when you eventually (and inevitably) uncover a diamond in the jewelry box.

It may seem daunting to think about, but trust me; it's easier than you think it is. In researching this book, I spoke with and interviewed hundreds and hundreds of women who have shared your experiences and frustrations and have come out of it strong, shrewd, and sensational—all of whom have *Been There, Done That, Kept the Jewelry,* and a few of whom eventually decided to tie the knot and make it official. You'll read their stories later.

The thing about dating is this: by common (albeit a bit cynical) definition, dating is a series of relationships that will either make it long-term or terminate. Those are your only two choices, and you can decide ahead of time which one you will be looking for. This book is for those who are looking for long-term. You certainly don't need help with the short-term stuff that will inevitably terminate. You can end relationships that aren't going anywhere all by yourself.

First and foremost, the goal is to get to know yourself better, and to figure out what your individual needs are in a relationship. This is not based on something that you've read, or heard, or something that has worked for someone else, but exclusive aspects of your personality that determine what you really need to be happy. You will do this by articulating your Essentials List, which are those little must-haves, also commonly referred to as "dealbreakers." We will figure this out together, remembering first and foremost that each aspect of your Essentials List is as unique as you are. Your list will be so specific to you that when you go out and meet a new potential Mr. Fabulous, any variation from your list that you detect in Mr. Not-So-Fabulous should absolutely send you running for the door. Now get those brand-new running shoes on, and let's go! Just as you would with a good home improvement, you will do a small overhaul of your mindset, or a renovation if you will. By fixing little cracks in your foundation and installing a "fabulous-man-seeking" device in your head, you will be able to figure out how to make the decision beforehand as to who is good for you and who isn't. That way, when you meet him, you'll recognize him. The first step is to become an expert in *you*. Maybe you've had some passionate and meaningful relationships with some of the men you've dated, but alas, they are no more. Now you wonder if there is a chance that you will ever meet "him." Well get that thought out of your pretty little head immediately! You will *absolutely* meet someone fabulous who is perfect for you. That's the key—not the "perfect" part, but the "perfect for you" part. Your Essentials List will give you a much better chance of dating the right guy from the very beginning and not wasting any more of your precious time trying to fix the unfixable. You will be able to figure out why you chose those awful men for magnificent you, and then learn how to spot the wrong ones earlier and move along more quickly.

Here's the most important thing to remember: You know full well what needs to be on your Essentials List, and you're also well acquainted with what your dealbreakers are. You've just never really looked at them in this way before.

In the workbook chapter we will teach you how to figure out what your Essentials are, step-by-step. The first step is to look at each of your past relationships and be honest about why they did not work. Which *Been There, Done That* guy were you with? Was he too immature? Was he a drinker? Insensitive? Did he not like Prada, or like it a little *too* much? Is there a recurring pattern in your dating life? If you can answer these questions, then you are well on your way! As you read each profile of the guys you may have mistakenly dated, I suspect some moments of glaring recognition will arise, and you may see some personalities that are all too familiar. That's a good thing—that's our goal. The idea is to have fun as you review these most common of guy types, but also to learn.

Remember, what is important is not so much who the *Been There, Done That* guys are, but who *you* are, and the reasons why you dated those different guys in the first place. The goal here is to gain some insight into yourself, and to use that information to figure out what your Essentials List will be. You will break it down and figure out what each guy may have represented to you. Some of your Essentials may include things that seem obvious, but the idea is that without them, your relationship will not work. That's the *real* secret to the Essentials List. It can—and will—predict your future.

After a date with someone new, you will be able to figure out whether he is right for you. You'll have your list of dealbreakers and you can be unbending with them, because you made that list before you went out with New Guy Number Seventeen. This way you won't edit the list to fit New Guy Number Seventeen's personality. Got it?

Keep in mind that your steps to finding your guy are exactly that—yours. It's all about you as an individual. You don't have the same needs as someone else, so you don't want the same kind of guy that someone else might. You have very specific reasons for dating certain kinds of guys. For example, some girls who date the Older Guy do so because their fathers weren't around and they want a father figure. You, on the other hand, may date the Older Guy because you are very close to your father, and the Older Guy reminds you of him. There may be father issues reflected in your relationship with the Older Guy, but you certainly aren't dating him for the same reasons as those girls who have absentee daddies. Sure, there are some universals and some generalizations that we can make, but the real story is always going to be a unique and individual saga. Only you can know your individual reasons for dating the guys that you have dated. You also know what is best for moving you forward, specifically toward the man you will eventually call your guy. You don't need a dating coach or relationship advice from everyone you meet. You already know everything you need to know about finding "The One." It's just a matter of doing the work and figuring out what it was about the *Been There, Done That, Kept the Jewelry* guys that attracted you so much, and *why* you fell for them when you should have kept the receipt and returned them posthaste!

With your Essentials List in hand, you'll be armed for any dating situation. The minute you encounter something that's a dealbreaker, then by all means, break the deal, girl! We need to move you forward so that any recurring thoughts of returning to those horrible men of your sordid past will stop *now*. Those men are not to be fixed, and they are not worth waiting for. One day they may be datable, but it will take years and years of therapy, and you don't have that kind of time! Why? Because your guy, the man who is totally worthy of your love and your time, is out there, right around the corner. You just need to go get him.

Before you go sprinting out the front door, though, let's see what we're dealing with. What are the profiles of men that any self-respecting Singlectual knows to avoid? Oh yes . . . read on.

PART ONE

the unattainables

women cannot complain about men anymore
until they start getting better taste in them.
—bill maher

These are the men who cannot be reached, achieved, accomplished, gained, succeeded, bested, or arrived at. They are, for one reason or another, impossible to attain. You may have read affirmations or inspirational quotes about the unreachable becoming reachable or something in that vein, but this isn't it. These are the men who, no matter what you do, no matter who you are, will always and forever be a waste of your time. Through no fault of your own, the Unattainables are inherently that, and are not to be conquered. ∿

chapter one
the bachelor

personality profile

The Bachelor has all the trappings of Mr. Right—charismatic,
exciting, and just the tiniest bit elusive, he's the type of guy
who always leaves you wanting more. The Bachelor's energy is
contagious. He is a risk-taker who loves the "extreme" version
of otherwise innocuous sports. I mean, why ride a chairlift up a
ski mountain when you could be heli-skiing into a ravine or cliff?
The Bachelor's social environment is instantly recognizable. He
has loads of single friends around him when he is out at a party
or at a bar and his eyes are always surveying the room looking
for a girl hotter than the one he just decided was the hottest
girl there. As the night goes on, "hottest" girl is downgraded to
"the girl most likely to go home with him."

At first glance, the Bachelor seems like a great catch

One of the men commonly encountered on any woman's journey to the altar is the Bachelor. Not to be mistaken for that hunky reality-show man muffin to whom fifteen hopeful women throw perfectly good perfumed G-strings, but instead a marginally attractive, self-serving, decent-seeming catch who has a way of making you feel like the only girl in the room. In a more pedestrian setting he is referred to as the guy who just won't commit, but his problems run much deeper than that. As my friend Shawna says, he is like a glass of water with a coaster . . . he never leaves a ring.

At first glance, the Bachelor seems like a great catch, as if he could in some parallel universe be The One. He will charm you and say he's in love with you after the first date, but ladies, beware! He is also the guy who will suddenly become a workaholic to avoid intimacy, hiding behind his busy schedule to avoid getting close and furthering your relationship. He will surely dump you by the second month. After a few missed phone calls and canceled dinners and several "Come over around eleven, I should be home by then" invitations, you start to realize that no one is that busy. Rather, the chase (a.k.a. the Bachelor's raison d'être) is over and you, my friend, have been demoted from dinner companion to booty call. At first you may blame yourself—you may think that you had sex with him too soon, or you should have waited before spending the night at his house—but none of this matters with the Bachelor. Unbeknownst to you, he stopped being interested in you the second you told him your name.

Take Amanda, for example. Amanda is freakishly picky when it comes to men. One night she was out with two of her more stuck-up girlfriends, ignoring men as they usually do. That night they were doing a great job of it. Men who sent them drinks or tried to catch their attention were snubbed all over the place. It was a stellar night . . . until she met James. It happened like this: Amanda and her girls were having dirty martinis and even dirtier conversation. It seems that Amanda's friend had just spent the night with a guy they all knew and she was entertaining them with stories of his extreme abilities in the sack when a cue ball from the nearby pool table came flying right into Amanda's mouth, breaking one of her teeth. A very handsome guy in a great shirt named James came running over to apologize for his friend's atrocious pool skills, and see if she was okay, when he realized that her tooth was badly chipped. As luck would have it, he was a dentist and his office was right across the street. This being James's local bar, the bouncer knew him and helped take Amanda over to his office for some late-night dentistry. Whether it was because of James' bedside manner or his incredible ass she can't say, but in

signs that your date with the
·· bachelor is not going well ··········

- ◆ He claims to be a sex fiend, yet he tells you, "let's be friends."
- ◆ You realize that the difference between a porcupine and his BMW is that a porcupine has its pricks on the outside
- ◆ When you ask if he wants to split an appetizer he barks at you, "Stop crowding me!"

any case, Amanda was very interested in having more than just her tooth fixed. After James fixed her up, she "thanked" him at her place. James seemed like a genuinely sweet guy, so after the thanking, the ordinarily cautious Amanda gave him her number.

To Amanda, things seemed to be going really well at first. Then, about two months into their relationship, James picked a fight with her on the phone when she asked him what he was wearing to a party they were attending. It was completely out of the blue! Amanda didn't really *care* what he was wearing to the party; she was really just asking out of curiosity. His response was not only shocking but totally inappropriate. Did the guilt he felt over breaking her tooth wear off? Why was he being so mean to her all of a sudden, over nothing? She decided not to see him for a few days to let him cool off and deal with whatever may have really been bugging him. A few nights later she walked past a restaurant with outdoor tables and saw him there on a date. Amanda thought that she had been dating a nice guy, someone who wouldn't just go and date someone else like that. She had always been so careful about who she let in, but now she feared that all along, she was dating the Bachelor.

It's a classic Bachelor move to pick a fight over nothing when you get too close. The Bachelor loves the game, which is why he is in the line of work that he is in (as explained in the Personality Profile that began this chapter). It's all a game—a man's game, at that—and you are just something else he's playing with.

Anyway, back to Amanda . . . sick to her stomach, she called him all night until he finally picked up the phone around 1 A.M. She felt like a fool, but she was hurt and she wanted answers. What Amanda failed to realize was that with the Bachelor, he doesn't feel

top ten items you will never see
···in the bachelor's apartment········

1. A toilet brush
2. Books like *Dr. Phil's Relationship Rescue* or anything with "How to Understand Women" in the subtitle
3. Paprika
4. An empty hamper
5. Matching dishware
6. More than one bath towel
7. A working hair dryer
8. Scented candles (or any candles for that matter)
9. Vegetables (V8 juice and ketchup notwithstanding)
10. The DVD of *The Little Mermaid* (he may, however, have *The Little Sperm-maid*)

the need to give an explanation so the last thing you want to do is confront him. It's like coming into a knife fight with an eyelash curler; no matter what you do, you are ill prepared. When Amanda confronted James, he was apologetic at first—not that he was with another girl, but that she had seen them together. Then he said those words that every woman who may be falling in love dreads: "We have to talk." And that was it—the relationship was over, with no reason, and no explanation. What had she done wrong? To Amanda, the way she and James met seemed like kismet; it was a funny and romantic story that she hoped to one day tell their grandchildren. You don't meet like that and then break up over an unceremonious argument! She, a smart, cynical woman in her thirties, was fooled by his charms. Her "jerkometer" was on the fritz and now she didn't know what to think. A few months later and no longer angry, Amanda ran into James on the street. He said he was waiting for "girl du jour." She was astounded by the phrase: *she* used to be "girl du jour." Now it was someone else's turn, some other unsuspecting woman who thought she was dating a cute dentist with a sexy butt. Her friends offered little in the way of advice because they didn't realize that Amanda was dating the Bachelor either—he was that good at his game.

Bachelor-isms

You will never domesticate the Bachelor. He's been down this road before and he will feed you excuse number 47 and sprinkle in compliment number 62 with reason-he-doesn't-want-a-relationship number 534. This will be especially true if he has been the Bachelor for some time, because that just means he is comfortable in the role. He's not looking for forever because he likes being a child himself; he isn't ready to have any of his own. Clearly, it is working for him; why should he give it up? Breakfast means swallowing a little extra Listerine by mistake, and asking whatever lady friend who happened to be there from the night before to make sure she closes the door on her way out. Furthermore, with people getting married later and later in life, this is the worst time to be involved with the Bachelor. We are all having extended childhoods, and the Bachelor is the worst of the bunch. He will never pay for a ring because he wants to maintain his amateur status. He likes his socks on the floor, boobs on his screensaver, and takeout four nights a week (the other three nights he eats what was left over).

·· ring-ring! ·····

You know you are dating the Bachelor when the phone call for a Saturday night date goes like this:

SCENARIO: *It's Friday after work and your phone rings.*

him: You want to have drinks tomorrow night?

you: Oh, before dinner or after?

him: After, ten. I have this business thing I have to do first.

you: Okay, what time are you picking me up?

him: Well, I was hoping you could just meet me, since I will already be out.

you: *(not happy about it)* Fine, see you tomorrow night.

If you were honest with each other, here's how that conversation should have gone:

him: Hey, I'm calling at the last minute. I thought I would see if I could ply you with cheap wine and then have my way with you tomorrow night?

you: You're calling me on a Friday night for a Saturday-night date? And you think I don't know that you're using me?

him: Well, there's this really hot girl I met, who I haven't slept with yet, but, you know, I'm working on it, so I have to take her for dinner first. Then I thought I would see you afterward.

you: Oh, so you have a date with someone else who is blowing you off at ten, so you're calling me to set up your booty call? Screw yourself, and I mean that literally, because that is what you are going to *have* to do this Saturday night. And don't ever call me again, you creep!

Speaking of socks, you will notice that the Bachelor is very inventive with his; he is the MacGyver of the sock drawer. Not that he has a pair that matches, but the ones that he does have, double as both coffee filters and napkins (hopefully not the same sock).

Still not sure that you are dating the Bachelor? Here are some tried-and-true clues to help you figure it out. The Bachelor is terrified of stuff like cleanliness and going to the doctor. He may say he's just "too lazy," but you know better. Those sandwich wrappers under the bed and clothes piled on his exercise bike, which you are *dying* to tidy up, scream out not to be touched! They are

in a nutshell

the fantasy After disappearing for six months he suddenly reemerges, realizing that you, princess that you are, truly are The One. Then you finally tame this loathsome beast as you walk away proudly with what is left of his ego dangling at the hem of your Valentino.

the harsh reality He has never had an honest conversation with a woman in his life and he believes deep down to his very soul that if you are interested in him you must have a fatal flaw. Which should be okay with you, because you will never stack up to his (pick one of the following) Mommy and/or Pamela Anderson fetish.

how you broke up He did it, actually. It was after you accidentally left an earring at his apartment and he said it was way too soon for you to be keeping things at his place. You never saw him (or that earring) again.

there to taunt you, in a way, to keep you from getting too close, because the minute you touch them is the minute he draws the line. He will walk around in pain for weeks just to spite you. His fear of the doctor is really about the proctologist; to him all roads lead there. The Bachelor is quite lethargic when it comes to stuff he really doesn't want to do. Oh, he has lots of energy for long golf weekends with his friends, paintball tournaments, boating trips, fishing trips, camping trips, or any other trip that involves male bonding and not you. Yet when he's home, the Bachelor has no time to get off the couch and come with you to a baby shower; he barely wants to put himself in his own shower. The Bachelor is an endless array of bad haircuts, empty refrigerators, phone numbers scrawled on little pieces of paper, bathtub fungus, unopened mail, and anything and everything that screams NOT GOING TO SETTLE DOWN and that you, my dear, are just his future ex. Unless you agree to bring a cute friend of yours to bed with you, you'll never extend your relationship with the Bachelor past its expiration date, which is usually at the three-month mark.

As a matter of fact, the Bachelor has a list of women he wants to date before settling down—if he ever does: The redhead who dumped his best friend; the hot girl in his office who drinks her Diet Coke through a bendy straw; the buxom Russian bartender at his favorite watering hole; the latest hot female race car driver; women of every race, height, and ethnicity; anyone who will sleep with him. If you learn the Bachelor's code you can tell if he's already dating them. You ask what he did last night, and if he had a date with another girl whom he took to a baseball game, he'll say he went to the game with a "friend." Then he will tell you all about how well Curt Schilling pitched. "Didn't do much last night" means he got kicked out of a strip club and spent the night in his car, while "Was out late with a bunch of guys" really means stayed up all night, ate an entire box of Mallomars, and watched *Goodfellas* for the twenty-fifth time. If you want the best advice about dating a guy like the Bachelor, ask the butcher at my local supermarket. He leans across the counter and yells, "Next!" Sharp and insightful, isn't he?

Why You Dated the Bachelor in the First Place

When I say "bachelor," what comes to mind? A cute, single guy who every woman wants? Or that creepy guy over fifty who calls his mother daily just to have some female contact? Statistically, the likelihood of marriage gets lower and lower as men approach forty, so staying the Bachelor for too long is not sexy. What made a sexy girl like you date him in the first place is of real consequence, especially if this is a pattern for you that you want to break.

At some point or another most women date men who cannot commit, because the fact of the matter is that some men will not commit . . . to you. Much of the time, that's how the sentence ends: " . . . to you." This guy will say that you are simply wrong for each other. If you are mixed up with the Bachelor, though, the real reason is that he is just in it for the game. The guy in Amanda's case likes the excitement of those first few months when everything was new and almost dangerous, but as soon as it starts to become a relationship, he's done. He's ready to jump ship and see who else is around, and he is insatiable. He'll leave bodies in his wake and justify it to himself as, "She wasn't the one, so why should I feel bad about dumping her?" If you let him know that sex was available during the time he had a passing interest in you, well, it was offered, so why turn it down? This answers that question about sleeping with someone too soon, doesn't it? If you know that a guy is on the fence about you, sleep with him because you want to, not because you think it will do anything for your relationship. With the Bachelor it never will.

A Part of You Knows Better, But . . .

Truthfully, though, going into why *he* didn't want *you* is so completely irrelevant. Who cares what he did and did not want? Our concern is why on God's green earth *you* would have wanted *him*? Why would you stay with any man who doesn't want you, and not run from him screaming in absolute horror?

First, the kinds of women who date the Bachelor are in some sort of cosmic contest with women across the world. "Let's see who can tame the wild stallion first," they say, and if it's you, then you win! Sometimes you may get so caught up in the chase that you are not even aware that this guy is so incredibly wrong for you. The Bachelor is great at that game—"I'll be just nice enough so she can fall for me, but then enough of a jerk that it keeps her on her toes." Or perhaps you have already invested so much time in him that the idea that he could be wrong for you is just a blip on your radar screen that you think is nothing to worry about, even though it actually is a huge monsoon heading your way.

Many times it's you who cannot commit, so you purposely choose a man who feels the same way about you. You choose him

if the bachelor went to a shrink
··she would tell him . . . ···················

At the extreme end of the spectrum, the reasons you and the Bachelor did not work out could just be circumstantial. You weren't the one for him; he wasn't the one for you; end of story. On the off chance that this is a pattern with the Bachelor—and there is a good chance it is—his shrink may diagnose him with Borderline Personality Disorder. His symptoms may include:

◆ *Efforts to avoid real or imagined abandonment:* This is why he will break up with you first, to beat you to the punch. That way he isn't vulnerable to you dumping him, which in his mind is abandonment.

◆ *A pattern of unstable yet very intense relationships:* These are the fun ones, because this is when the Bachelor loves you to death and idealizes everything about you. Then, when he is alone, he convinces himself that he's too good for the likes of you, and what the hell was he thinking? Moments later it's back to "my lord, she's a goddess!"

◆ *Chronic feelings of emptiness:* This is the Bachelor you never get to know because privately, this is what he is feeling.

◆ *Identity issues:* The Bachelor doesn't have a good sense of self. His insecurity shows itself when he has to remind others how fabulous and accomplished he really is. By doing that, he is reminding himself. He tells the waiter, "Since I am the president of my company, I do have some say as to where my clients eat when they are in town, so make sure you give us special treatment." One thing is true about *The Bachelor:* when he has to let everyone in the room know of his accomplishments, he's a loser. And if you are intuitive you may pick up on this, but you have to be on your game. The Bachelor would never actually *tell* you that he feels this way.

- *Mood swings:* Oh, Mr. PMS, here we come! You know how you have grumpy days during that time of the month? Well you have hormones to explain yours; what's his excuse?

- *Inappropriate anger:* He's mad that you ordered tomatoes on your sandwich, he's mad that there was a rain delay, he's mad that his cat ignores him. It makes no sense; he's just mad. And there's nothing you or the world can do about it.

Now you see that when the Bachelor dumps you and your ego is bruised, you have to snap out of it! Realize that you had nothing to do with it, and in his eyes, you could have been anyone. To him you are no different from any of the other girls he may have dated. He didn't get to know the real you, now, did he? You thought he was a decent guy but you missed the signs, and now he's off with another girl who he will dump in three months. It is a blessing to rid yourself of the Bachelor, especially if he is the Bachelor because he has major psychological problems. Quite frankly, if he doesn't want to be with you, then he must have major psychological problems anyway!

because he is unavailable, or because he reminds you of someone in your past who treated you terribly, and you have to right that wrong, or simply because you just like the game too. And if you do, that's fine, but just be honest about it. Life is a set of choices, so just make sure that you always make the best ones for yourself, because nobody else is going to do that for you.

Take Erica, for example. Erica is forty-two, and dating a guy who keeps telling her that she isn't the one and it's just a matter of time before he finds someone else, yet he keeps taking her on vacations, spending lots of free time with her, and calling her nearly every day. She says that she likes the attention, but the reality is that they have been together almost a year and he is still looking—just not at her. You're probably asking, "So, what the heck is she waiting for?" I keep asking her the same thing, especially when she admitted she wants to get married. Erica claims she doesn't know why she stays with him. "Chemistry and great sex" has been her answer in the past, but the hurt and heartbreak that is coming her way cannot be worth a good shag.

What is really happening here is that deep down, Erica doesn't feel that she is worthy of being treated the way she *wants* to be treated by the man she loves. She feels guilt over past relationships and this is her mea culpa: she doesn't deserve real love and is punishing herself by dating men who treat her poorly. So, she's trapped in this situation because she's not ready to be real with someone. "Real" equals "pain" in her book—and with that frame of mind, who *would* be ready to be in a "real" relationship? If you, like Erica, like the game, and are staying with a guy even though he's telling you that you're not The One, just make sure that you are being honest with yourself. Know that it's only a matter of time before the Bachelor is true to his name and goes back to his terminally single ways. He knew the minute he met you that the relationship was going nowhere; did you? That is the main issue here.

You should be sick of being treated as anything less than the fabulous woman that you are, and you should want more. It's time to make the break, find the strength, figure out what your Essentials are, and tattoo the list to your arm because you are going to need it. (You'll learn all about creating your Essentials List in Part Four of this book.) The fact that you are dating the Bachelor says a lot more about you than it does about him. Why wouldn't you ask for more for yourself, and more of the men that you date? You do deserve so much better, and The One is absolutely out there somewhere, no question about it!

 *your jewel of wisdom*

You've certainly learned something by doing time dating the Bachelor. What precious jewel of wisdom did you take away from your sordid time with him? It is this prized lesson that will help you put together your best possible Essentials List. Start thinking critically about your relationship. What was it about him that won you over in the first place? Now that you have come to your senses, what have you learned? Maybe *you* were the one who didn't want to commit. Or did you just want to date someone who was a challenge to you? Perhaps you're a "Miss Fix It," looking to turn him into the good guy that you're just sure is lurking deep inside of him. If you can pinpoint exactly what it was that was so alluring about him, you are well on your way to shaping a valuable Essentials List.

chapter two

the hot guy

personality profile

This shouldn't be too hard, because it isn't really about his personality, now is it? If it were we would call him Quantum Psychics Guy or Sweet, Sensitive, I Really Wish I Liked You Guy. One of the draws of the Hot Guy is his sheer lack of personality. So when you are at a laundromat and there is a gorgeous slab of man meat celebrating breaking even at the change machine, that's your fella.

So pretty—if only he could form a complete sentence

You always wondered what it would be like to date one of those *really* hot, living, breathing, Ralph Lauren ad guys, haven't you? Your opportunity comes along when the Hot Guy takes a shine to you in a bar that has two feet of beer on the floor and Kool and the Gang coming out of the speakers. You think to yourself that you indeed are something special, and that this specimen of loveliness really gets you. Maybe that's been your problem all along—you were aiming too low. Those average-looking guys who treated you like crap were just intimidated by your effervescence, and this hunk-o-rama totally gets it. "Finally!" you think to yourself. You've been vindicated! You decide to date the Hot Guy because, well, he's really hot! It's also because you need a break. You need a break from having to be witty and clever, and you need a break from having to talk about your family, dreams, hopes, goals, and desires. The Hot Guy doesn't care about that sort of thing. He's too cool for talk (or he really just doesn't understand the words—you're not sure and, either way, you don't care).

Just don't start planning the seating chart yet or picking out china, because while he will look great in a wedding album, you might be better off to consider the Hot Guy as the cute waiter your bridesmaid hooks up with and not as the groom. Alas, while the Hot Guy is just too pretty, he is also just too dumb. Yes, he looks great in jeans, but don't even consider taking him out of the house because his incredible beauty will ruin all chances of other men approaching you. Why? Well, two reasons, really. First, he is prettier than you and second, he will intimidate even the most

a history of dating
in the beginning

If you are feeling overwhelmed at this point, or if you are just overwhelmed in general about dating and relationships, here is something interesting that many women find quite inspiring. It is a brief history of dating and marriage in America, and its purpose is to help you realize how far we've come, and how good we have it, now that we have a choice in the matter. You'll find these sidebars scattered through the chapters.

Dating and marriage has changed a lot over the decades. What started as an institution of convenience and practicality has evolved into partnerships based on love. Did you know that marriage originally was mostly about men finding hearty women who could bear children, work farms, and take care of the house and their land? This means that in colonial America, Kate Moss would have been a spinster, while Roseanne would be a highly sought-after temptress. Ah, to live in colonial America and be able to eat all the carbs and cookies you desired . . . anyway . . .

secure guy. However, his personality is limited to a rambunctious tête–à–tête about hair products and duct tape, and if he calls something "ironical" one more time you'll go off the deep end. (In truth, though, you are so busy looking at him you hardly even notice.) The good news is that you can train him to do everything that you like. The bad news is that he has a mind like an Etch A Sketch. If he looks too quickly to the right, all of that precious information is lost in that lovely head of his.

Virginia met her Hot Guy at a party one night in October. She introduced herself amid the loud music, he thought she said her name was something else; they had a laugh about it. At first she could not imagine that this man of utter splendor would be interested in her. When the conversation turned to how many Gummi Bears each could eat in one sitting during a major munchies attack, how could she not leave with him to go find out? He was very, very hot, and Virginia could not believe that she was doing so well with this guy. Mid-bear, he asked for her number. When he called the next day to see what she was doing for Halloween, Virginia told him, "Oh, we're not very into it, so my roommate and I are having our own little Bah-Humbug night." So why was she surprised when he showed up with six buddies in Hawaiian shirts, with leis and piña colada mix at 10 P.M. on October 31? "What are you doing here?" she asked. "Oh, aren't you having a Bahamba party?" he said excitedly. "No," she explained, "Bah Humbug . . . like Scrooge." The blank stare told her that he had no clue what she was talking about. She wondered where he thought "Bahamba" was anyway. No matter, he was there and gorgeous. She knew in that moment that she would one day tell that story to other women, who would nod their heads in sad familiarity. You may be doing that at this very moment.

Hot Guy-isms

Maybe you met the Hot Guy at your local college bar or some other cool hangout where being pretty gets you in the door. Perhaps he crashed a party near your school, but don't mistake him for a classmate; he doesn't go to your school, or any school for that matter. He simply lives in the area and plans on taking his GED. Everyone tells him that he should be a model and asks him why he is wasting his time going from job to job. It's true he should do that while he is still young and so, so pretty. If only he could figure

··· **ring-ring!** ·······································

You know you're dating the Hot Guy when the phone call for a Saturday night date goes like this:

SCENARIO *It's Friday morning. Your phone rings:*

him: Hello?

you: Hello?

him: Hello?

you: HELLO!?

him: Who's this?

you: *You* called me!

him: Oh . . . hey . . . how are ya?

you: (inquisitively) Good? How are you . . .

him: Oh, I'm okay . . . Oh wait, I have a call waiting . . . Hello?

you: Still me.

him: Hello?

you: Still me.

him: HELLO!?

you: (*hang up*)

If you were honest with him, here's how that conversation should have gone:

Your phone rings, you check your Caller ID, and see it's him. You let the machine get it.

out how to read a train schedule and get to a nearby city—those confusing timetables with their numbers and codes! The Hot Guy is such a vision that you hardly hear what is coming out of his mouth. It's moving and he's looking in your direction and that's all that matters until he shows up for your first date. You open the door and . . . oh yes . . . he is as divine as you remembered! Your first inclination that something isn't right with him is when you walk into the restaurant, look at the menu, and exclaim, "I'm famished!" to which he replies, "Oh really, my last girlfriend was Catholic." And you don't correct him because you would hate for him to get those frown lines from trying to understand.

Then somewhere between a conversation about his first dog and deciding to split the flan for dessert, it occurs to you that he has nothing to say. He doesn't read the newspaper and couldn't care less about world politics. When you tried to talk about current events, he said that he always thought it was so odd that George Washington, Christopher Columbus, and St. Patrick were all born on holidays. Check, please!

Maybe your Hot Guy had some other fantasy element besides the obvious one. Perhaps he was a surfer with no job, or a carpenter with no job, or was in some other Hot Guy profession that didn't actually require him to work. This was your opportunity to escape the real world—the real *dating* world, that is. Hot Guy isn't like the rest of us; he doesn't have to worry about getting enough vitamin B12, or about global warming. His world is much simpler, and that is the main reason behind your attraction to the Hot Guy (the cheekbones and sexy butt thing aside.) He gets better service for no reason, free drinks from female bartenders, and everything else afforded to him on the "free stuff for Hot

·· in a nutshell ··············

the fantasy Hot Guy will go back to school, get a Ph.D. in physics, win the Nobel Prize for inventing a perpetual motion machine, fly you in his Learjet to your high school reunion, and cure cancer, all before they serve the mini quiches.

the harsh reality He couldn't spell Ph.D. if you spotted him the "P" and the "h." He also thinks mini quiches *cause* cancer.

how you broke up You took him out and yelled "Look over there," and then you ran. He is still looking over there.

Guys" program. This is your chance to see how the other half (or, more appropriately, the other 1 percent) lives.

Nevertheless, you have been in a dating slump with worse. At least he will look good at that birthday party for snotty little what's-her-name next Saturday night. Fendi on one arm and hot man muffin on the other, you'll show her. But he's a lot like the mirror that he constantly gazes into: pull back that layer of silver and there is nothing there but a piece of transparent glass. This is the bitterest pill to swallow as reality hits. He isn't your dream man but instead a man you once had a wet dream about. This doesn't make for good husband material. After all, Hot Guy doesn't marry you—he marries Hot Girl (ask your guy friends, they'll explain).

Why You Dated the Hot Guy in the First Place

Right, like we have to really analyze this one. Ummm . . . 'cause he was *really* hot! Well, that is part of the reason; after all, who are you to deny anyone of your company, especially the physically gifted yet intellectually challenged. But each one of us knows that every once in a while we need our egos stroked. We are not made of stone, and when a really hot guy finds us attractive, it is an ego boost to even the most secure among us. We feel exonerated from the wrongful dating choices of our torrid past. It's an in-your-face to the less-hot loser we dated before him, who made us feel worthless. And if we can parade Hot Guy past the ex, all the better. Dating this trophy boy is our Golden Globe during sweeps week, our grand slam during a batting slump, our Gucci purse in a five-dollar-sales-bin moment, and we are thankful.

The problem with dating the Hot Guy sets in when you don't think of this as a temporary relationship, but try to make this man,

top ten items that hot guy uses
to make himself hotter

1. Baby oil
2. Vo5 hair oil
3. Body oil
4. 0W40
5. Astroglide
6. Wesson oil
7. Mineral oil
8. Cod liver oil (he likes to keep his *insides* clean and "hot" for you, too)
9. Omega 3 fish oil
10. Deodorant (all that oil makes him stink)

who is not intellectually on your level, higher on your dating priority list. A few years back there was an e-mail going around of a gorgeous, gorgeous woman, and in tiny letters scrawled across the bottom of her picture it said, "Believe it or not, some guy out there is sick of her shit." Though the e-mail was meant as more of a crass joke than a moral lesson to uphold, there is some truth to it. This e-mail was a harsh reminder that physical beauty isn't as lasting as we think, and—sorry to be corny—the beauty inside a person is what you should really be attracted to. That's not to say that beautiful people don't make amazing mates, but in some cases (and I know this is hard to believe; there is research to support this), extremely beautiful people have an easier time getting what they want based on their looks. This tiny percentage of the population has had less asked of them in life, and as a result, are not as motivated to achieve much beyond aesthetic beauty. Of course, there are many, many intellectually gifted, successful, gorgeous men out there. But when it comes to the Neanderthal hunks that we love to call beefcake, it's best to refer to them in hindsight only, never in present tense. Stunning as they are, they are not worthy of you.

A Part of You Knows Better, But . . .

Take Robyn and her Hot Guy, Tyler, for example. Robyn always had a thing for the model Tyson Beckford, so when she met Tyler in the park both his name and his strong jaw (as well as his dreamy eyes) reminded her of her man Tyson. She was there with friends playing touch football and having a picnic when Tyler's cousin began hitting on one of Robyn's friends. Robyn would never have

if the hot guy went to a shrink,
·· she would tell him . . . ···············

The Hot Guy is perfect just the way he is, at least to look at. But ya gotta wonder about a guy who has nothing upstairs and is perfectly happy getting by on his looks. That "I don't have to try, I just am" thing can really chap your ass at times. What is so great about the Hot Guy anyway? If he had enough substance he wouldn't be just the Hot Guy, he would be a real catch: a gorgeous guy with brains, personality, ambition, *and* hotness.

So why is it the Hot Guy is just the Hot Guy and nothing more? His shrink may say that he is a classic case of Narcissistic Personality Disorder. His symptoms may then include these:

◆ *He has a grandiose sense of importance:* He thinks that beauty is all he needs and further, that he has achieved something because of it, as though "pretty" amounts to something more than "pretty."
◆ *He has crazy, crazy fantasies of ultimate beauty and power:* Somehow he thinks that hot equals success. If he were a model, that would make sense, but he carries that attitude even if he isn't on the runway.
◆ *He believes he is so special, he can't really be understood by mere mortals:* The Hot Guy is only good mixed with the

Humble Hot Guy; otherwise he's just obnoxious, thereby becoming the Insufferable Hot Guy.

◆ *He has a sense of entitlement:* The world (and you) owe him something because he is just SO beautiful. The Hot Guy thinks he should be treated differently, or actually *better* than everyone else (including you). Unfortunately, he *does* get treated that way, which only reinforces his sense of entitlement.

◆ *He takes advantage of others:* He uses his powers for evil, and not for good. Because he is so hot, people like to do things for him. Instead of getting them to give money to charity, he gets them to give money to Charity, his favorite stripper at Scores.

◆ *He has no empathy:* He doesn't care about starving children or sick puppies, and there's no way he's volunteering with you at a soup kitchen on Thanksgiving Day—he has a massage scheduled (nor does he care that his masseur wanted to be with her family)!

◆ *He believes others are envious of him:* Well, if he *really* is the Hot Guy, then they actually might be. But this isn't something you want to encourage if he is a narcissist.

◆ *He's arrogant and haughty:* See all of the above.

imagined in a million years that a guy as incredibly gorgeous as Tyler would ever be interested in her, but he came right over to talk. He seemed to like how smart she was, and kept proclaiming it over and over: "I love smart women." "Oh, I see you're one of those intelligent-type girls, I dig that." Tyler claimed that his IQ was 20/20, and while Robyn recognized immediately that she was in the company of persona Hot Guy non-grata, she decided to pretend that it was okay with her. She was more impressed with herself for being able to garner the attention of such a beautiful man than the reality of his glaring limitations. For the moment, his broad shoulders overshadowed all else.

Tyler asked for her number and then called the very next day. Robyn was now enthralled with the idea that he was so into her that he could not wait to speak with her. "Those hours in kickboxing class must have started to pay off," she thought to herself. So what if he was dumb as dirt? Tyler liked Robyn so much that when he found out she was vegan (and after he asked her what that meant), he said that he was going to be vegan too. About a month into his vegan ways, Tyler went with Robyn to a "Walk for Farm Animals" event to raise money for the Farm Sanctuary. He knew that she was really into saving all kinds of critters, as well as into the environment, and all kinds of other charitable/noble causes. Her enthusiasm inspired him to do something charitable, too. Tyler's big moment came when he noticed that despite the deer-crossing sign posted on an area of the nearby highway, many deer still got hit by cars and trucks. Tyler decided to take matters into his own hands, and marched into the local department of transportation office to ask them to move the sign to a safer area. Robyn's first thought upon hearing his tale of triumph was that if he wanted to help her raise money, he would have been better off posing shirtless with a chicken for a calendar. Smart girl that she was, she never would have suggested such a thing, for fear that he would show up on her doorstep with a bucket of KFC. Robyn dreaded the thought that her relationship with the Hot Guy was over, but she could no longer put up with all the jokes from her friends (like the time they suggested he go to the fridge to get the dehydrated water). The final straw came when Robyn and her friends were sitting around one day, and somehow the War of 1812 came up in conversation. Not surprisingly, Tyler told her later that he didn't contribute to the conversation because he wasn't quite sure when that war had taken place. At that moment, Robyn knew that it was goodbye. The moral of the story is, you date Hot Guy for your ego, and that is perfectly fine—just put an expiration date on that fine ass of his and you'll be okay.

your jewel of wisdom

Well, you thought you had a diamond with a few rough edges this time. Turns out he was just a very sparkly rhinestone. Ask yourself what you have learned—there's no point in loving and losing if you can't come out of it stronger and smarter. Did you like the attention of such a handsome man? Or did you just like feeling smarter and superior to someone so beautiful? Or maybe you liked the simplicity of being with him and having very few consequences to your actions? Think about what it was about the Hot Guy (other than his obvious hotness) that you were truly attracted to, and see if you can put that on your Essentials List.

chapter three
the older guy

personality profile

The Older Guy is a great guy. He's the first guy you've encountered in quite some time who *isn't* a jerk, which makes him very attractive after dating so many of them. The Older Guy is looking for a woman to treat like a queen. If he was on Oprah and she asked him, "So, what are you looking for in a woman?" her audience would "Awwww" with every description of the wonderful life he is looking to give his lady. He's your dream man. Unfortunately, he comes in a flabby, aging package. At twenty-five he would have been perfect. Then again, at that age he was probably one of those jerks, and you were . . . well, not born yet.

Everyone knows that women mature faster than men

When you first meet the Older Guy you are convinced that this is the relationship you have been waiting for—after all, everyone knows that women mature faster than men. You fancy yourself wise beyond your years and the Older Guy must be looking for a wise woman, right? You can *finally* have a partnership and a relationship with no drama. The Older Guy is good at making you feel special, virtuous, and worthy, and for a while, he even gives you the illusion that you are being treated as an equal. Think again, though, sweetie, because on some level the Older Guy thinks you are silly and young, and he likes being the Older Guy because whether you want to admit it or not, he's got the upper hand. He never had the upper hand with his wife. This is his karmic retaliation; he finally gets to call all of the shots, *old dog new tricks my ass*, he thinks. The Older Guy may even have kids, which means that he resents your biological clock and won't even talk about being a father again; it's where he draws the line. Yet, thanks to modern technology, Older Guy has the perfect pill; it's made up of ginkgo biloba, Viagra, and Prozac. The pill helps him remember how to do it, aids him in actually doing it, and then alleviates the guilt afterward.

The Older Guy may rush you into bed before you can say father fixation. Physical malfunctioning aside, sex with the Older Guy can be good because he has had lots and lots of experience and knows exactly what to do and better yet, what not to do. No more directing oral traffic. Guys your age need a tutorial before getting into bed with you, but not the Older Guy. He's got his technique down to a science, really. Once that relationship starts to turn sour, though, all of those great hours in bed quickly turn to "Who's this old guy?"

Take Mariah, for example. She was a total party girl who usually ended the night with some dating nightmare brought on by beer goggles, hers mostly. Being the devoted party girl she was, she made sure to befriend the bouncer, Jack, at her favorite club. He was a gorgeous, muscle-bound hunk and a half, and some sixteen years older. But Jack took care of her and that made him special. He made sure she had drink tickets, got in free, and often called a cab to take her home at the end of the night. Mariah had never been babied like this before and thanked Jack in the best way a party girl can: she took him home one night. She describes her relationship with him as a one-night stand that

top ten items in the older guy's apartment
···· that are older than you are ········

1. His favorite pair of underwear
2. The expiration date on his milk
3. His cat
4. His computer by Texas Instruments
5. His Ma Bell phone
6. His Pan Am travel bag
7. A Time-Life Books series on the Civil War
8. The photograph of his first wedding
9. His Flash Gordon decoder ring and Gigantor figurines
10. His sense of outrage

lasted six years. Mariah noticed almost immediately that in many ways she was much more mature than Jack was. He was in his forties and "totally didn't have his act together," she recalls. He

a history of dating

the dark ages

While love and respect was supposed to develop eventually over the course of time, sexual attraction and romantic love were never the basis for wedlock. The bride's father and the groom's father had the legal right to give consent, or to withhold it. The fathers would get together ahead of time and have a sort of summit meeting to negotiate terms before the engagement was formally announced. The bride usually brought her dowry into the marriage, which consisted of everything from household goods and clothing to money. The groom provided the land, house, and tools for his wife to use as she labored on his behalf. Could you imagine your father sitting down with his father now to negotiate the "terms"? Maybe they should, and maybe it should be more like this: Your father says, "We request a shopping spree at Bloomingdale's once a month with no repercussions, and we request no sports metaphors in relation to any conversation, particularly those involving their sex life." His father says, "Done. Providing we receive seats to the Super Bowl annually, and a no-nagging zone, which includes her refraining from all wardrobe criticism as well as criticism about his friends, his mother, and the way he asks from busboys what he should have requested from the waiter." "Done, announce the engagement."

didn't save money or plan for his future but instead lived paycheck to paycheck. "He was basically a forty-something-year-old kid," she admits. Since Mariah was in her early twenties and "wasn't looking for anything crazy," it just kept going till one day she just outgrew him.

Jack was extremely immature and irresponsible with his own life, as many Older Guys are, but despite neglecting his own responsibilities (like seeing his children), he treated Mariah as a daddy would, as many Older Guys do. Jack always had meals in the oven when she got home, paid most of her bills, and gave her guidance. However, Jack partied like he was in his twenties, except that unlike guys who really were in their twenties, he always had money. Since Mariah grew up without a father, this arrangement suited her nicely. Jack would rent limos when they went out and he would pick up groups of people Mariah's age. Jack and Mariah had limo parties that would last till dawn, and the scary part was, Jack fit right in. Mariah recalls one super-duper party that he had for himself. "It was his 'thirtieth' birthday party," she recalls. Mariah asked him why "thirty," considering that he was turning forty-five. Jack told her it was because he had never had a thirtieth birthday party. But she suspected it was because nobody knew his real age and since they were all so much younger, he wanted them to think he was actually about to turn thirty.

Mariah was never more aware of how old he was than when he injured his knee. During his long rehabilitation she was eerily aware of all of the medical difficulties ahead because of his age. What if he gets an aneurysm or a blood clot or has to have major knee surgery? She didn't think she wanted to be caring for the

Older Guy when there was so much more partying she had to do. This was a wake-up call.

The Older Guy can have arrested development, like Jack, which means he's got the body of the Older Guy but the mind of a nineteen-year-old. Or he can be more like Foster, who at forty-six was madly in love with Pam, who at twenty-eight knew that she was in charge. She told him right from the start that she wasn't looking for anything serious, and he rewarded her by taking her to Paris, on the most romantic trip she had ever been on. Maybe *that* would win her over. Then, when she told him she wanted to see (a.k.a. have sex with) other people while also seeing him, he bought her a diamond bracelet. Then when she called him to pick her up at 3 o'clock in the morning from a one-night stand, he rented a chalet and took her skiing. Foster was lovesick and just happy to bask in the glow of this very lovely, very young thing. While Pam took advantage, Foster looked like an idiot . . . but an idiot who had a twenty-eight-year-old on his arm. He was willing to be treated terribly just for the pleasure of her company, and that made him feel young and superior, especially when they went out with his Older Guy married friends. Foster loved the look on the faces of his forty-six-year-old friends (and their forty-six-year-old wives) when he brought Pam around. Poor Foster; he didn't realize that the look was that of pity, not envy.

Older Guy-isms

The Older Guy is such an easy mark, and while it's disturbing and weird to the rest of the world, he can be a very good daddy to you.

·· ring-ring! ··········

You know you are dating the Older Guy when the phone call for a Saturday night date goes like this:

SCENARIO *As usual, it's Wednesday when your phone rings.*

him: Hey, just calling to see what you had planned for Saturday night.

you: Nothing, I'm free, just in case you wanted to take me to Paris!

him: What?! Who says I dress garish?

you: No, that's not what I said. Never mind, I was joking.

him: Oh my God, should I call 911?

you: No, why?

him: Didn't you say you were choking?

you: No, never mind. How's about we catch a late dinner?

him: Oh late, huh? Okay, I guess I'll pick you up at six o'clock then.

If you were honest with him, here's how that conversation should have gone:

him: Hey, just calling to see what you had planned for Saturday night.

you: I actually do have something planned. I'm going out with men my own age. I'm sick of having dinner at lunchtime. I hate that while we're out the waiter asks me if my father would like some more decaf, and I just cannot look at your saggy ass in your mirrored ceiling one more night.

He may not have a ton of money, but what the Older Guy has he is willing to throw your way. Pam got Foster to pay her rent the month she was short, and when her car broke down, he took it to get it fixed. Just reading this, doesn't it seem totally un-cool and pretty pathetic to date someone for his wallet and for what he can buy you? Doesn't Pam seem like a sad gold digger? Are you wondering if she has any self-respect? You should be. This wasn't a fulfilling relationship for either of them; it was just one big waste of time. Life is WAY too short to waste precious dating years, especially your hot ones, on such a superficial existence. It is just sad.

Even if you are not dating the Older Guy for his money, this isn't usually a situation in which you will really learn any profound lesson about life. It's just for fun—and sometimes it *can* be fun to be with the Older Guy, like when he takes you antiquing and to restaurants you couldn't afford. It is hard to get him to try new things, like that overly trendy sushi restaurant you kept insisting on going to, owned by that famous actor guy. The Older Guy doesn't eat sushi. Don't you know that the Older Guy feels like why should he pay, if nobody cooks? At first your generational differences were cute. You showed him how to work a PlayStation 2 and a BlackBerry; he taught you Pong on Atari and how to work an abacus. No matter, at least Older Guy comes pre-trained. You don't need to tell him to call on Wednesday for a Saturday-night date, he knows not to flirt with your friends, and he won't ask you to meet his parents—they're dead.

After a while, all of those differences that made him (as you told your friends) "really mature" start to become creepy. For instance, you loved his alternative jewelry choices until you

·· **in a nutshell** ···············

the fantasy You go to dinner with George Clocney.
the harsh reality You wake up with Sean Connery.
how you broke up You moved to a sixth-floor walkup.

realized that Older Guy's idea of bling-bling is his heart monitor and a MedicAlert bracelet. You loved reading the paper together on Sunday mornings—it was just so sophisticated—until you realized that while you went to the Weddings section to see your friends, he went to the Obituaries to see his. You worry about being hip; he worries about breaking one. He knows 4 bits, you know 50 Cent. You just got sick of having to explain that Lil' Kim is not a midget in a Korean circus. The thrill was gone.

Why You Dated the Older Guy in the First Place

Just when you thought it was safe to jump back into the dating pool, along came the Older Guy. He may not have been the hottest guy you dated, but there was something about him that felt right and maybe even a little bit dirty. Like that time when you met him in a hotel room and the next day he bought you a fabulous necklace. It wasn't prostitution per se, but it was as close as you were ever going to get, and it felt daring. You never did the sex-for-gift-exchange before! But you thought, "You know what? Someone should take care of me!" It was such a drag dating all of those guys who couldn't really spoil you as you had always

signs that your date with the
··· older guy is not going well ··········

- ◆ He says that a daytime date can lead into the night only if you just let him go take a "disco nap."
- ◆ You are whispering sweet nothings in his ear and he says, "Wait, let me turn up my hearing aid."
- ◆ He goes to kiss you goodnight and his breath smells like an autopsy.
- ◆ You begin to describe dating him as being like two hypochondriacs waiting for the doctor to call.

fantasized about. Now you were dating someone who could spoil you either the way your daddy did, or worse, the way he *never* did. More than just spoil you with gifts, the Older Guy spoiled you with attention. He never competed with you, he was not threatened by you, and there wasn't much of a challenge to get and keep his attention. While this seemed fine at first, it is not the basis for a lasting relationship. The Older Guy may act young while you are first with him, but the truth is that he isn't. As the newness of your relationship fades, so will he, as will your patience for your differences. Don't even get me started on dating married men. Suffice it to say that I guarantee he will not leave his wife for you, and even if he does, he will cheat *on* you just as he did *with* you. Before we even continue, let's all agree that we are talking about the SINGLE Older Guy. No more wasting your time, okay? The main point is that a crush on the Older Guy should stay just a crush; life (especially his) is too short to wait for him.

A Part of You Knows Better, But . . .

Often women will date the Older Guy because they find themselves being treated differently than they've ever been treated by men their own age, and they like it.

Amy is a theater producer who started dating older men when working on a series of regional theater pieces. Suddenly, she found herself surrounded by older men. Everyone from the other producers, to the director, and even some of the actors were all at least fifteen years older than she was. It was the first time she had spent so much time around this many older men. Despite the discrepancies in age, Amy felt respected and treated as an equal, and she liked it. Amy began to seek out older men to date, theorizing that, for the independent woman who wants to take care of herself, it's the perfect relationship: The Older Guy knows who he is, there are no games, and her independence never felt threatened. Amy was doing fine with older men until she met, and fell hard, for Charlie, who was twenty-two years her senior. Amy openly admits that she has a father thing going on, so it was no surprise to her friends when she started dating Charlie. At first everyone thought they were cute together (if not *weird*), but after about ten months her fantasy love faded away. One day Amy looked across the table and realized there was an old man sitting across from her. He was crazy about her, and now she was about to break his heart because, after the va-va-voom faded, they had nothing in common.

In many cases, women will date Older Guys who have themselves been there, done that. The main problem with those Older Guys is that they aren't interested in getting married again. Hey, this breed of the Older Guy is jaded. He has kids and ex-wives and feels like he's paid his dues. While he isn't quite ready to hang it up completely, he is also not looking for anything permanent with you. He's had all the "new" experiences there are to be had: he's been to the Caribbean, he's tried parasailing, driven cross-country; he's done all that already with his exes or his kids. There are no more firsts for him. Let's be honest—the Older Guy is a little selfish. He feels as though he's been a good father, a good husband, a good employee, and now he just wants to have a rocking good time, and put himself first. He may even want you to sign a palimony agreement if you suggest living together. He doesn't really care about your feelings, and your wants and needs are not his priorities. *He* is his priority, and he feels like he's earned it.

And though it may not seem like a big deal at the moment, if you are with the Older Guy long enough, you will inevitably have to face the fact that the Older Guy gets even older. This means that, at some point, your relationship will change and you may have to be a caregiver. Now, for some women, this is an opportunity to finally take care of a guy the way you always wanted to. Where guys your age may have labeled you "needy" or "a doormat," the Older Guy sees you as nurturing. After all, who else will rub his bunions just right? He's kinda cute now, when he's forty-two and you're twenty-seven, but what about when he's sixty-two and you're forty-seven? Will you be interested in taking care of him then? Are you willing to possibly face widowhood in your fifties?

When you first start dating the Older Guy, you rationalize it to your friends by telling them how perfect you are together because everyone knows that men are slower to mature, so it's like you're the same age emotionally. You not only like his emotional maturity, but you also like the security that he brings you,

if the older guy went to a shrink
she would tell him . . .

First off, that she isn't a proctologist and he can pull his pants up. Oh, Older Guy and his forgetfulness! If his BMW didn't have keyless entry he would never get anywhere. At first you thought it was cute when he put the milk in the pantry, and kinky when he forgot his dentures before your date. But after a while spoiled milk and the ineffective gumming of steaks begins to take its toll on your patience. The shrink will tell you that Older Guy has Age Related Cognitive Decline. Not sure? Here's how to tell:

- *He exhibits decline in cognitive function commensurate with the aging process:* In other words, his mind is going. He has turned the corner from great sage to old age.
- *He can't remember names or appointments:* The Younger Guy forgets your name because he's a flake or just stoned; Older Guy has no bong to blame. Don't despair—he can't remember his own name, either.
- *He has difficulty solving complex problems:* He always forgets whether it's two spoons of Metamucil or one per glass of water.
- *There's nothing neurologically wrong with him:* His issues do not root from a problem that's some kind of brain thing. Really, he's just suffering from a case of O-L-D.

unlike those exciting tumultuous relationships of your past. Lust and passion are for the young. With the Older Guy, passion may have died after the first or second night but dammit, your rent will be paid and the chia pet he got you will be watered! But hold on a second—it sounds like, while you were busy rationalizing, you forgot that you were looking for an equal, and that what you really deserve in life is love, not just a bank account. Sure, you *say* that the Older Guy won't hurt you and that he is teaching you so many things, but in the long run, he is just too old! You won't be comfortable with someone that age ten years from now, will you? You can still respect your elders; just stop dating them.

your jewel of wisdom

The jewel you take away from your misadventures with the Older Guy has strong sentimental value, like the vintage brooch willed to you by your great-grandmother. You grew up turning it over in your hands, enchanted by its history, which has always seemed so much bigger than your short little life. It's a one-of-a-kind piece, they don't make them like they used to, and you'll cherish that brooch forever—but it doesn't exactly go with your Pucci scarf and your Blahnik slings, now, does it? Your stint with the Older Guy didn't work out for the exact same reason: you want someone you can grow old with, but the Older Guy, like great-grandmother's brooch, has already grown old without you. So, what were the qualities that attracted you to the Older Guy that made you feel safe, loved, and cared for? These qualities, in a more au courant package, will undoubtedly increase the value of your Essentials List.

PART TWO

the uninspired

the way i see it, if you want the rainbow,
you gotta put up with the rain.

—dolly parton

The next group of men are damaged, tired, and uninspired. In the lackluster dating life that you have created with them, they might run the gamut of wearing their pain on their sleeves to never letting go of yours. This was your moment of slapdash dating, when you threw something together in the form of temporary companionship and then you just hung around because there was nothing better going on (or maybe he wouldn't let you go.) In any event, the Uninspired will guarantee you a life of uncreative and unoriginal dating experiences that will leave you unmoved, uninterested, and unimpressed. Take any word that you love, put an "un" in front of it, and there he is. ∾

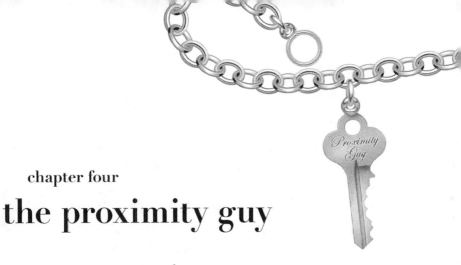

chapter four

the proximity guy

personality profile

The Proximity Guy's personality is not as important as is his locale. He could be a nice guy or he could be someone who doesn't pay his taxes, cheats at poker, and hates all references to kittens. You don't know. It's easy to spot him, though. The minute you are feeling sexually deprived, rejected, or are simply having a low self-esteem day, he is the lucky guy who smiles at you in the elevator or asks if you want to "supersize" that, and for a brief moment your worries are gone. In other words, it's all about you, baby. Who cares about *his* personality?

Do you like him? Or do you just need something off that high shelf?

The Proximity Guy is the guy you date because he happens to live in your building/dorm/neighborhood and he's available. Maybe you saw him moving in, so you brought him a basket full of cheese, fruit, and condoms. After all, you wanted him to feel welcome. The Proximity Guy serves several purposes for you. He's the guy you go out with until something better comes along, or because you just don't feel like being alone on a Saturday night, or because you need something off a high shelf. Whatever his function, the most important aspect of the Proximity Guy is that you don't care how he feels about anything real. His opinion is useful for such questions as, "Does this look too slutty?" when dressing for a date. Beyond that, the relationship is all about you. You don't worry about saying or doing the right thing with him, and what a relief that is! It's nice to be in a relationship (if you can call it that) with no expectations and no consequences. The Proximity Guy is your dating get-out-of-jail-free card. You don't want to meet any of his friends or his parents, nor do you care to listen to his problems at the office. Why he didn't make partner is of no concern to you.

The Proximity Guy is best put to use as the guy you date on the side while you are trying not to fall for another. You know, that really cute guy you just met and are trying not to obsess over? Those nights when you are tempted to call but you know you shouldn't call, or you are wondering why he *hasn't* called, and any other issue relating to calling, e-mailing, or texting with the guy you *really* want to date? Well lucky you, now you can suspend

signs that your date with
proximity guy is not going well

- He begins a sentence with "I've said it a thousand times before . . . I'm straight!"
- During your date he excuses himself to bus the table.
- At dinner he interrupts your conversation by answering his cell phone with "Why yes, I would like to hear about a new long distance plan."
- You ask what movie you will be seeing and he says, "Well, I'm seeing Revenge of the Nerds Eight, what are you seeing?"

all of those concerns by going over to the Proximity Guy's place. It is your safe place.

With the Proximity Guy, you needn't be subtle. It's okay because he isn't subtle with you, either. You both know that your relationship is going nowhere and you take comfort in the idea that not every guy has to be your soul mate. You see him with other women and recommend restaurants for them to check out. You ignore his birthday and don't feel bad about it. The only time you insist on cooking for him is when you are trying out a dish for the guy you *really* like. The Proximity Guy is a great guinea pig for many things. Wanna try some weird sex thing, like moaning a little too loudly or using some unusual props, perhaps? Well, here's your big opportunity. The Proximity Guy is up for anything.

Bridget had just moved to a new city and didn't know a single soul. She was feeling lonely, and away from all things familiar.

Mike seemed to come out of nowhere at the perfect time. He lived next door to her and when he cornered her in the produce section of their local supermarket, she was charmed. Mike's sudden appearance fit into a fantasy Bridget always had of being swept away by a sexy stranger. Mike insisted on being her tour guide in her new city, which soon led to a tour of his bedroom. Bridget said that while Mike was probably dating two other girls in their building, she liked having someone to occasionally share a pizza and her bed. The best part was, she didn't have to do anything and didn't ever have to try. It was easy; he was just there and it was all so convenient. She knew that she didn't love him, but she enjoyed the attention. "I like attention," she said. "Who wouldn't?" Bridget recalls how insensitive she was to him, yet she

top ten items in Proximity Guy's apartment
·· that you had no idea he had ·······

1. The exact same set of takeout menus that you have
2. His high school yearbook picture . . . framed
3. Plaques and awards for doing noble things like Big Brothers and cancer walks
4. A roommate
5. A Saint Bernard
6. Two priceless Warhol paintings
7. Roof access
8. A last name
9. A sex swing
10. The Holy Grail

cannot explain why, because she isn't normally that kind of person. However, he didn't really seem to care. She remembers one day when some total hottie flirted with her at work, her boss praised her for something she had worked hard on, the sun was shining, and she felt wildly optimistic about the world. She saw Mike that night and exuberantly exclaimed, "I really think I'll meet someone special this year!" Within a month or two she made some friends, found a better apartment, and moved, not even giving Mike a second thought. "It was just over, for me at least." Mike could be someone's Wounded Guy right now (you'll learn about him in the next chapter), but most likely, he has found some other temporary girl to hang out with for three minutes.

Proximity Guy-isms

The beauty of the Proximity Guy is that he doesn't have to live next door to you. He also might be that guy you see at company functions and make out with in the coat closet. You know those times when you've had too much Chardonnay and you just want to suck face? The situation calls for the Proximity Guy. You know those nights when you get stuck working late and you want a dinner and a shag? Sounds like a job for the Proximity Guy. You know when you get canceled on at the last minute or stood up on a blind date and you are all dressed up with no place to go? The Proximity Guy is your man. He is the all-purpose utilitarian man. They should bottle him.

You can consider yourself especially lucky if you've hit the Proximity Guy jackpot and he is a hunky dancer at Chippendales,

···in a nutshell ················

the fantasy The Proximity Guy will somehow morph into über-boyfriend and lo and behold . . . marriage.

the harsh reality He needs to shave his back, get a different job, get rid of that old futon, ditch his lame friends, lose the '80s acid-wash wardrobe and Duster, learn how to better spend his paycheck, bathe his dog, realize that Buffalo wings are not a major food group, open an IRA, get rid of his beer bottle collection . . . sheesh . . . too many changes. Just date someone else.

how you broke up You never "officially" broke up, you just stopped going over there, pretended not to see him in the hall a few times, and once called him by the wrong name in the laundry room.

or has some rough-and-tumble dream job where he spends his day lifting things and getting sweaty. Any type of job that you would never consider for a real boyfriend job can be considered a great Proximity Guy job—maybe a phone sex guy, or something really awful like a reality show conflict manager (a.k.a. the one who writes the trashiest scenes for his unsuspecting reality TV cast). You and the Proximity Guy can have hours of fun playing out those fantasies, writing some wacky circumstances of your own. Or better yet, maybe the Proximity Guy is Santa at your local mall. C'mon, like you never had *that* fantasy.

Take heed though; you have to be clear that there are major don'ts with the Proximity Guy. Don't introduce him to your friends or anyone who has access to really great men with whom

they'd like to set you up. Don't take him to any family functions. Don't discuss him with your hairdresser or be seen with
him in public alone, only in groups. You don't want to give the
message to anyone around you that the Proximity Guy is anything special. And finally, don't worry about all of these don'ts
because you will not hurt The Proximity Guy's feelings—he's got
his own game going on. There will be moments, however, when
you briefly fantasize about the Proximity Guy meaning more to
you. "Perhaps I've been too hasty," you think. Then you roll over
and take a gander at his hideous taste in shoes. "Tassels?!" you
think. "How excruciating, what is he, in boarding school?" And
you are snapped back into reality.

Why You Dated the Proximity Guy in the First Place

Well, duh . . . proximity! It's right there, in the chapter title! But
it's more than that. Were you bored? On the rebound? What was
the *real* reason that you dated this person, who is so totally not
your type? So not your type that you knew all along that one day
you'd look back and laugh at the fact that he remained on your
dance card for so long? Your criteria for dating someone has to be
more than "he lives close by." It's okay if he was just a stopover on
your way to the next guy, as long as you don't delude yourself into
thinking otherwise. Look, not every guy you date has to be The
One, and that is the main point of the Proximity Guy.

The Proximity Guy is your "what if" guy, the guy who filled
in the blank when you asked yourself, "What if I dated _____?"
Maybe you never dated a musician and hey, there's a drummer

who just moved in down the hall from you. Why not go find out how good he is with his sticks? Or maybe he worked on a project with you at work and you thought, "Hey, I know doing it in the paper closet is a cliché, but what's life about if not living out fantasies before you tie the knot? We'll photocopy our butts too; let's go for the whole clichéd office romance proximity package!"

When Tabitha moved to a small town for work, her Proximity Guy was Gavin, a divorced man with whom she did business. When he moved his office into her building and came up for a face-to-face, she gave him a mouth-to-mouth. She wasn't really interested, just bored being new in a small town. Gavin was cute enough but more important, he was there. I asked Tabitha what else happened in their relationship, but true to the Proximity Guy dynamic, the story ends there, really. Tabitha met her Proximity Guy, they dated for a few months, and once he stopped calling, she never saw him again. End of chapter. Tabitha likens it to eating Twinkies when you have PMS—they taste damn good at the time, but when you're feeling better you realize that they are weird, artificial, and just not that satisfying. Definitely not worth the extra pound or two you put on by eating them. What a terrible waste of calories when you could have been savoring a decadent chocolate truffle.

The Proximity Guy can also be called the Experimental Guy. You'll do things with the Proximity Guy that you would never do with a real boyfriend because you know it's just a (pardon the pun) layover. Did you ever want to have a threesome? Do it in a restaurant bathroom? Remake a man from head to toe, then dump his ass? Well, that is precisely what the Proximity Guy is for. He's the guy with whom you share an unwritten code that your relationship isn't going anywhere, and you are both fine with that. He is the sacrificial dating lamb and you don't feel bad, not one iota! The Proximity Guy wasn't serious about you either, and took it all in stride. As a matter of fact, he immediately moved on to another girl at the office. He sees her when he is not with the girl who lives downstairs from him. You see, he is a serial proximity dater. All the convenience with none of the wear and tear on his tires, his speedometer, or his footwear, terrible as it is.

A Part of You Knows Better, But . . .

The point that you are missing is that the Proximity Guy was essentially a waste of your time. You dated him because you felt that you had to be with *somebody*. *Somebody* is better than *nobody*,

ring-ring!

You know you are dating Proximity Guy when the phone call for a Saturday night date goes like this:

SCENARIO *It's Saturday night, and he sees you coming in early from a bad date.*
him: Wanna come up?
you: Sure.

If you were honest with each other, here's how that conversation should have gone:
him: Wanna come up?
you: Sure.

Since the Proximity Guy was never going to be The One, who really cares what his shrink would say? Just for fun, lets examine the kind of guy who lets himself be someone's Proximity Guy. Perhaps he has a social anxiety disorder, or what a clinical shrink may refer to as Avoidant Personality Disorder. Social anxiety is pretty much what it seems: social situations make him feel anxious, because the Proximity Guy fears being rejected, laughed at, not liked, or any combination of those. Avoidant Personality Disorder is a bit more specific than social anxiety. If the Proximity Guy has Avoidant Personality Disorder it will look like this:

- *He avoids activities:* Perhaps he even fears them, specifically the ones that make him feel he will be criticized or rejected. Being in a relationship with no consequences is right up his alley.
- *He is unwilling to get involved with people:* That is, unless he is certain he will be liked. If you sleep with him, I think he can be pretty certain that you at least *like* him.
- *He shows restraint:* This does not come into play with anything good, like having too much dessert after a big meal, or purchasing too many superhero figurines. In this case, the Proximity Guy shows restraint with you by not getting too

close and basing the time he spends with you on . . . you guessed it, proximity!

- *Inhibited and inadequate=indoors!* Yes, that is why you do a lot of your Proximity Guy dating in Proximity Guy places. He is a bit socially inept and is really not a fan of things like the outside world.

- *He's usually reluctant to take personal risks:* Oh, he may bang you on the kitchen table, but he would never do anything bold, like change careers to follow his dreams, or do something better with his life. You know, something that might actually keep you around. It's that last point that may drive home why the Proximity Guy never gets very high on your list. You are dissatisfied with so many things about him—so many, many things would have to change if you were ever going to take him seriously—but his reluctance to take risks or engage in a "new" behavior will always keep him from doing all that stuff he needs to do that would move him from the Proximity Guy to major boyfriend.

right? Wrong. These types of relationships, where you are with someone just because he happens to be nearby, are the ones that may inevitably leave you feeling worse. You have to admit that on some level, even though you were not interested in the Proximity Guy in any real way, you still wanted him to want you, right? (Cheap Trick reference notwithstanding.) Not that you would have done anything about it, but it would have been a nice ego boost. The fact that he didn't fulfill that wish is damaging because at some deep level, you wonder why a guy who you couldn't care less about doesn't want you. Your self-esteem is not something to amuse yourself with. You need to distinguish between guys who you want to like you for purely selfish reasons and guys who you want to like you because you have given them reason to. You didn't give the Proximity Guy any real foundation to start falling in love with you. Not falling for you was part of the deal initially, so don't start pretending that you care how he feels just to enhance your ego. Why would you all of sudden give him the power to hurt you? You got into it with the Proximity Guy because you were done with pain; you needed a vacation from that stuff.

Now you can see why a relationship with the Proximity Guy wasn't the brightest move. The time you spent dating the Proximity Guy could have been time spent doing things to boost your self-worth, not damage it further. This could have been time spent getting closer to a friend who has been there for you in the past, or to a relative who could really use a little extra attention from someone right about now. Barring all other scenarios, this was time you could have spent getting to know yourself better. It's okay to be in your own skin for five minutes without a man in your life. Women who don't date the Proximity Guy are the ones who find real peace in being with themselves. Every relationship that you are in leaves its mark on your psyche in some way, even the "meaningless" ones. You never get to walk away unscathed, even if the damage amounts to feelings of guilt over lost time that you could have spent doing better things with your life. Wouldn't you rather look back on this as the time that you finally went to London, or the time that you started writing your screenplay, or, even better, the time in your life where you did nothing at all and you were okay with that?

 *your jewel of wisdom*

The Proximity Guy was like a flawed diamond. Ask yourself, what was it about being with such a flawed individual that fed you? It's true that on the surface he had lots of great things about him, but whatever you do, don't look at him too closely or you will surely be disappointed. You certainly will never take him out in public, and you will also never be completely satisfied. The good news is that when you make a lot of money one day, you will be able to afford an upgrade, but how will you know the new guy will be worth it? That is your Essentials List, which will bankroll you into a better stone in the very best setting: your life.

chapter five
the wounded guy

personality profile

When Wounded Guy is in his normal state, which would have been the state he was in before he met "the Ex," he may have been a good guy—or, he may have been any one of the other guys profiled in this book. That is because many of them, given the right combination of unfortunate circumstances, can become the Wounded Guy. So your concern cannot be with whom he might have been, or even the potential as to who he can become, because the Ex changed all of that. He has now taken a different path. You have to look at the Wounded Guy in the present only, and right now he is an open wound, vulnerable to life, yet angry at it in the same moment. He's dangerous to date because he isn't stable. Anger isn't stable and extreme neediness isn't stable. No matter how you look at it, you're doomed.

In a year (or ten), the Wounded Guy could be a truly great catch

The Wounded Guy just got out of a very serious relationship, or maybe just hasn't gotten over his last big romance. Either way, he isn't ready to date yet. That didn't stop him, though; he has decided to bestow his misery on the rest of the world. While most people take some time right after a breakup to figure it all out, or go to counseling to work out their issues, the Wounded Guy has innocently, yet cynically, chosen to date before he has fully recovered from his last relationship / divorce / first love / bad childhood.

This is really a bad-timing situation more than anything else. In a year (or ten), the Wounded Guy could be a truly great catch. Right now, though, he has so many unresolved issues that he dates like a zombie. He talks incessantly about "her" and tries to use your relationship as a means to understand why-oh-why she dumped him. The Wounded Guy doesn't need closure so much as he needs a sledgehammer to the head. You choke back anger as he goes on and on about the woman who just broke up with him, comparing her to each and every woman he has dated in an attempt to trace his footsteps back to where it all went to hell. You think to yourself silently, "Get off the cross, Jackson, someone else needs the wood!"

Claire had that very thought, over and over, as she listened to Eddie try to "reconstruct" the whole scenario with Betsy, his ideal woman, who had just left him for another guy. When Claire used the word "reconstruct," I thought she was being facetious, but she said that Eddie only wanted to go to places that he and

Betsy had been, sit where they sat, and—no joke—have conversations just like they did. Eddie once asked Claire to say, "One day our kids will thank us for raising them in this city," just as Betsy had said, while sitting near the Bay together. When Claire didn't say it exactly the way Betsy did, Eddie gave her the correct line reading. "It was like some twisted, bizarre Civil War reenactment," she told me. She wondered when Eddie was going to break out the Betsy costumes for her to wear. Why did Claire, a sane, wonderfully datable thirty-five-year-old, put up with this? She said that Eddie seemed to have no real friendships, and it made her sad to think that he was alone. Eddie was ruggedly handsome and she could not imagine that this pain would go on too long, since he seemed so manly. When he didn't snap out of it in nearly eight weeks, she moved on. Eddie probably didn't even notice. He may have been the Wounded Guy, but that also made him a completely self-centered jerk. When you are out with the

a history of dating
the wild west

By the mid-1800s people were moving westward, and women were scarce in these newly settled territories. The best a man could do was to import a woman from back East, or to place a personal ad in a newspaper for a wife. Some of the ads for women back then were for those who could raise children, knew their way around a skillet and a hunting knife, and could sew britches. Today WWCP might mean White Woman, Catholic or Protestant; back then it meant Woman With Coffee Pot.

···ring-ring! ···························

You know you are dating the Wounded Guy when the phone call for a Saturday night date goes like this:

SENARIO *It's Tuesday night. The phone rings.*

him: I was calling to see if you want to get together this week.

you: Great, how about Saturday night?

him: No, no, can't do Saturday night, it's the anniversary of the day that Sara and I broke up. Well, the night she broke up with me actually. I should start to acknowledge that, right?

you: Okay, what about Friday night?

him: *(gently weeping)* Nope, can't do that either, that's Sara's birthday. I know I'll spend the night wondering if I should get her a gift anyway. Should I? Maybe I should.

you: Well, then let's have dinner Thursday night.

him: *(now in full crying mode)* Oh no! Thursday night is the anniversary of the night Sara and I first went bowling. She was so adorable . . . *(dial tone)*

You have hung up by now and are sure that he didn't notice.

If you were honest with him, here's how that conversation should have gone:

him: I was calling to see if you want to get together this week.

you: Okay, fine, but if we go out this week here are the rules. No mention of Sara's name, no crying, no requesting the songs "Sara" by Jefferson Starship or "Sara Smile" by Hall & Oates. No reminiscing or asking advice of any kind, and any breaking of these rules will result in immediate end of date. You got me?

him: Oh . . . well, some other time then. *(Click)*

Wounded Guy you are never really alone, because "she" is always there with you in his mind (maybe even when you're in the sack with him, and you are not into threesomes.) But if you're really lucky, maybe you'll land a Wounded Guy like Wendy did. Her Wounded Guy made an odd decorating choice. He had two boxes of "her" things in the middle of his living room, like a shrine. He would sit and stare at the door longingly, like a three-legged dog at the pound anxiously awaiting a new home, sure that she would return for them. Wendy realized that as patient as she was, this was a lost cause. The upshot is that the Wounded Guy learned a lot in that last relationship: he learned how to be sensitive, how to listen, and how to care. But in the end, he also learned bitterness, anger, and resentment. Those last three wonderful traits are the ones he will bring to you.

Wounded Guy-isms

The Wounded Guy tends to be a little chatty—like "the FBI might be on his tail" chatty—no matter how stoic he may have been in his former state. A guy who would not admit to being moved when they rescued Baby Jessica from that well, or Elian Gonzalez from his inner tube, will suddenly talk endlessly like a Teddy Ruxpin Bear. Why did she leave him? What did he do wrong? Will nobody ever love him for him? God, it's almost like dating another girl.

The good thing about all of the Wounded Guy's talking is that it offers insight for you into who he is and how he's feeling every minute of the day. Your ability to understand why she dumped him can be useful information. You can see if he really is a great guy who just chose the wrong woman, or if he's a creep who got what he deserved. Are you a rebound, or just another ex in the making? Or is there more to your relationship with the Wounded Guy? If she cheated on him, that tells you something very different than if she ran screaming because he was driving her crazy (see the next chapter, "The Clingy Guy"), or worse, because he was atrocious in bed. These are things a girl needs to know ahead of time, not the type of thing you want to find when it's too late. His incessant exploration of why his wife or girlfriend left him gives you the upper hand. You have become the pack leader, the alpha wolf. Whatever you say goes, and your opinion is sacrosanct. He will hang on your every word.

The downside to dating the Wounded Guy is that now you have to figure out if he's just a mama's boy who plays the role of Wounded Guy in every relationship. Everyone has luggage, but did the Wounded Guy overpack? If so, you have to wonder where the Wounded Guy got his dating education. You have to consider that his only source may have been his loser older brother or a socially inept friend who gave him terrible advice. This means that he was a Wounded Guy waiting to happen, and your job is to make sure he isn't happening to you. Of course now that "she" rejected him, she has become the gold standard, the perfect women that you will never live up to. He will have sex with a vengeance, then leave you wondering if you did something wrong in bed. Yes, honey, technically you did; you chose to date the Wounded Guy. Your bad.

Still not sure if you're dating the Wounded Guy? A telltale sign is if he casts you in the role of Mean Mommy. You know

top ten items wounded guy
·· has hidden under his bed ··········

1. Love letters to his ex jammed in a shoebox
2. CDs from The Cure and The Smiths
3. A yearbook with women's pictures circled with notations like "Could have" and "If I see her at the reunion"
4. A pristine unopened box of engraved engagement announcements
5. An emergency case of Jim Beam
6. An unopened box of condoms circa 1998
7. His diary
8. Girls' names and numbers scrawled on napkins that all turn out to be from the DMV or Joe's Deli
9. A box of dead Valentine's Day roses he never sent
10. A papier-mâché heart with a knife through it that he uses as a visual aid during arguments

this one; it's the game where you whip him into shape with some tough love while your sad little whipping boy feels deserving of your harsh treatment. He has become a social masochist who feels that on some level he deserves to be treated badly. Don't reprimand him; he'll secretly like it! Under no circumstances are you to recommend a spanking—you don't want to encourage him! Just to be on the safe side, though, check your state's battery and sexual deviance laws.

One final note about the Wounded Guy is that there is a good chance that he could also just be damaged. This doesn't necessarily have to be from his latest breakup, but could instead be due

··· in a nutshell ············

the fantasy Plenty of desperate lovin'.
the harsh reality Plenty of desperate lovin'.
how you broke up You took him to ladies night at McDrinky's, gave him a condom, and said "Good luck."

to a recent death in the family, or some other traumatic event that has impacted his life. You may choose to be a comfort to the Wounded Guy, and give him something more than just a condolence card—like a sympathy lay. But please be forewarned: If Wounded Guy is mixed with pity sex, it might cause Clingy Guy (and probably drowsiness, too.) Warning: Do not operate anything while heavy petting. If indeed you overindulge the Wounded Guy with pity sex, see bartender immediately.

Why You Dated the Wounded Guy in the First Place

Make no mistake, you are the quintessential rebound and the Wounded Guy will transfer all of those lost loving feelings onto you. You will be the best thing that has ever happened to him—until he sees the real you, which may not be for a long time because frankly, he isn't looking. You have to know that he is not seeing you for you, and has instead projected all of those feelings for his ex your way. You are the substitute teacher in his classroom of life. Look closer and you will see why he isn't worth your time. It's clearly all about him: his needs, his breakup, his feelings. You began the relationship on unequal footing. Need proof? Take a look at his behavior. Classic Wounded Guys never initiate any social activity, even when it's called for (your birthday, for example.) With the Wounded Guy, you know instinctively that you cannot count on him, so you don't even ask. Not only is the Wounded Guy rebounding from his last relationship, he is rebounding from all the hurt that he has had over the course of his lifetime.

You date the Wounded Guy because you secretly like the one-sidedness of the relationship. While he tells you everything about his life and struggles to figure it all out, you remain a mystery. Perhaps you always wanted to be mysterious to a man, but the Wounded Guy is not the person to explore that with because, in the end, he doesn't really care about you. The reason the Wounded Guy isn't asking about you is not because he wants to take his time and get to know you slowly, or because he likes the secrecy and anonymity of you; it's because he *really* isn't interested.

At first you are attracted to the Wounded Guy because you are sick of dating men who can't talk about their feelings, and who never want to be close. Now you're with a guy who will tell you *everything* that he is feeling, and may even tell you, within the first month, that he loves you. Don't for a second think that you aren't lovable, because you most certainly are! However, you can't ignore the fact that the Wounded Guy doesn't see you for who you are. These intense feelings he seems to be having for you are not coming from a sincere place; they are simply postbreakup feelings, and he has nowhere else to put them. Ask yourself, what are you going to do if she wants him back? You know he'd run back to her in a second. His big secret is that he is looking for a girl just like the one who married dear old Dad—or worse, a girl who can live up to that unachievable perfect wife/girlfriend ideal he has in his head.

Most of the women I interviewed who dated the Wounded Guy came from very stable homes and thus felt equipped to deal with the repair duties required when dating the Wounded Guy. Girls who are a mess themselves could never handle the Wounded Guy's crap. They are too involved with their own issues to be an ear for the Wounded Guy's abundance of troubles. True, many of you Wounded Guy daters grew up with great parents, but then again, you are used to living with the mutts your mothers brought home from the pound, the cat that wondered into your backyard, or the cockatoo that was willed to your family from the guy who sold you the house. If that's the case for you, it stands to reason that you would date the Wounded Guy, because you learned early to take in strays. Furthermore, you looked at all of the Wounded Guy's problems and were sure that you could fix them. Think about it: Though you may feel just a glimmer of recognition while reading about the Wounded Guy described in this book, haven't many of your guys been damaged in some way? And wasn't it always the case that you thought that your stability and good sense would somehow save them?

A Part of You Knows Better, But . . .

The guy that you dated who had the seriously crazy mother, or that socially phobic guy you went out with, were all Wounded Guys in disguise. These are the guys you figured would be willing to look at their issues and even go into therapy once they got to know fabulous you, so they could finally enjoy a healthy relationship. You thought that you could change them. Finally, they would see that to have the phenomenal relationship you were offering, all they had to do was make one little personality adjustment and poof, they would find instant happiness. What you failed to realize is that all of those Wounded Guys out there just don't see it. They are so mired down in the muck of their own crises there is no way they would truly recognize loveliness such as yours, let alone the gift of stability that you tried to give them. You were so wonderful and understanding and tried very hard to be what you thought the Wounded Guy needed. Unfortunately, it just didn't happen.

Juliana thought it would be fun to date an actor she met, who was working on a television show. He didn't have a big role or anything, but he was on regularly. He was cute but not too cute, smart but not condescending, and totally humble about being a working actor. She thought she had quite a catch on her hands, and soon she found herself making plans to move in with him. ("Soon" meaning within three months of knowing him.) They looked at several apartments before settling on one that seemed just perfect. Juliana

signs that your date with
... wounded guy is not going well ...

- ◆ As soon as you see him your first thought is, "We don't thin the herd as much as we used to."
- ◆ On your way to the movie of his choice he stops to buy not a small pack but a two large boxes of tissues—one for each of you.
- ◆ As he is telling you yet another endless story, you have but one thought: decaf.

if the wounded guy went to a shrink

···she would tell him . . .···············

There is no question that the Wounded Guy could be just your run-of-the-mill guy who has simply had too many bad breaks, but if your Wounded Guy is having yet another repeat performance of "why didn't she love me," a shrink might just say that he has depression. If he has a majority of the symptoms on the list that follows, no amount of Ben and Jerry's will shake him out of it. You need to suggest professional help and then move on, fast, like a psychological ring-and-run. Start running if any of these describe your Wounded Guy:

◆ *His usual mood is dejected, gloomy, joyless, and generally unhappy:* When that sad puppy-dog thing isn't cute anymore, like after a week or two, you may be dealing with a very wounded Wounded Guy. Which begs the question, why would you want to hang out with someone who is such a stick-in-the-mud?

◆ *His self-concept is in the toilet, and he feels worthless:* Does all of that poetry about death and doom make you think he is just a tortured artist? A lost soul? No sweetie, he's just a mess.

◆ *He blames himself and is derogatory toward himself, guilty and remorseful:* The irony here is that you like being right, but after a while it's just like shooting fish in a barrel.

◆ *Pervasive pessimism:* He's got sad cow disease.

went home to decide which furniture was going and which was going into the trash and called her actor to see what he thought. After several days of unreturned messages Juliana started to think his behavior was odd, and she began to worry. Then, finally, when he called her, he broke it off. What Juliana didn't know was that she had a Wounded Guy on her hands all along. And he was the worst kind of Wounded Guy, the one who came bearing wounds from childhood and never did anything about it, but instead took that damage from relationship to relationship. "My family is exactly what he needs," she thought to herself. She had a stable, loving upbringing, which she knew was the prescription for what ailed him. She was rescuing another stray. Juliana expected that he would recognize this was what he needed and be the wonderful boyfriend she had been grooming him to be. Instead, when he dumped her she never saw it coming. The moral of this story, ladies, is that the Wounded Guy is as socially self-destructive as a wrecking ball run amok. Your best bet is to just get out of its way.

your jewel of wisdom

There's no question that the Wounded Guy is a big old mood ring. No value, but sort of a fun novelty piece that you thought you would try on for size. As it changed moods, you went from amused to bored, till finally you just shoved him in a drawer. So . . . how did you do? Were you a good listener, or did his neediness drive you mad? The way you handled the Wounded Guy, and the appeal of him in the first place, is your jewel of wisdom, the most priceless part of a worthless piece.

chapter six
the clingy guy

personality profile

When you meet a guy and he is a great listener, that's a good sign. When he wants to hear your life story the night you meet him, that's a sign that he may be the Clingy Guy, and that's bad. Beware. It's not that you aren't fascinating, because you most certainly are. The problem with the Clingy Guy is that he has very little moral fortitude, would never ask for what he really wants in any mature way, and is looking for a woman to take over for him. With too much time on his hands, he focuses on bizarre hobbies, such as making sock puppets out of socks he finds in his laundry room, or collecting Starbucks memorabilia. When you first start dating him, make sure you don't tell him your schedule; he will figure it out soon enough, so he can turn up when least expected. That's his new hobby (next to groveling for sex).

He's cute enough—but my God, he's driving you nuts

The Clingy Guy (not to be mistaken for the Klingon Guy, that *Star Trek* freak you dated the summer between high school and college) is a lovely, wonderful, sweet, sensitive guy who really wants to be with you *all the time*. He's really into you; you're just barely tolerating him. At first you think, "Damn right he's into me—who wouldn't be?" Finally someone is treating you like the worship-worthy goddess that you are. Is it so wrong that you wish he'd just shut the hell up for five minutes about you meeting his mother? No, of course not—considering this is only your second date. The Clingy Guy is also obsessed with talking about the trip you'll go on next summer, or what his sister said about the two of you because they "just talk about you all the time!" You pray that, for one brief second, he'll stop trying to hold your hand at the wrong time, or touch the small of your back as you walk. You may be able to grin and bear it now, but somewhere deep inside a part of you is on the verge of screaming, "Oh my God . . . get your hands off me and get a life!" He's cute enough—but my God, he's driving you nuts.

It's sad, really. So much potential that was obviously meant to be enjoyed by someone else. As a matter of fact, you have thought of all the great single women that you could set him up with once you've rid yourself of him (although he may drive them bonkers, too). The problem here is, he likes you—he really, really likes you. And while you want guys to like you, you don't want them to like you at the exclusion of everything else in their lives. He is the human equivalent of a puppy. Let's call him the man-puppy, a tiny, yappy puppy that if you weren't such a humanitarian would

a history of dating
·· 1940s–1960s ·····················

The sexual revolution that took place during the mid-twentieth century was primarily due to the increase in premarital intercourse, which on many levels mirrored the beginnings of the women's movement and made arranged marriages a thing of the past. When we stopped referring to each other as "Sir" and Ma'am" we began snogging and shagging full speed ahead. The Great Depression saw a decline in marriage because it was fiscally impossible to begin a new household together; you stayed at home as long as you could with Mom and Dad. It was not really until World War II that marriage rates began to climb again. Between 1940 and 1942 there were one thousand marriages a day! Cut to the 1950s, when weddings became big business and thus bridezilla was born. It wasn't too long before feminists everywhere began to criticize the institution of marriage as sexist and unfair, which caused marriage and dating to take yet another turn. In the early 1960s women started dating men whom they had no intention of marrying, and sex became something that you didn't have to be married to do. Not to mention the introduction of the birth control pill, which ushered in the age of sex for recreation and not procreation. However, interracial marriage was another dating hurdle that we had to endure, and it was not legal to marry outside your race in many states until the late 1960s!

love to give away. He'll go to chick flicks with you, or the mall, it doesn't matter; he is your man-puppy, and will follow you anywhere.

Quinn met Omar online in a chatroom where people were talking about African safaris. Quinn couldn't decide between elephant tracking in Samburu or an African lion expedition in Zimbabwe. Omar seemed to know a lot about African lions, so they struck up a friendship. On their first date, Omar was extraordinarily smitten with Quinn; he said that he felt an "instant connection" with her and that their mutual interest in Africa was a "sign." Quinn thought this was a bit weird, considering they'd just barely met, but he was adorable with his big sad eyes, and while he wasn't the type of guy she normally went for, there was something kind and sweet about him, if not corny. Despite the fact that Omar overwhelmed her a bit with gifts like a little beanbag lion and a framed map of Africa, she agreed to a second date, which he secured before dessert.

The next day, when she had a minute to review the night, Quinn wondered, "When did guys' biological clocks start ticking louder than ours?" Omar looked as if he was on a wife search, not a dinner date. To Quinn, the date felt more like the Spanish Inquisition then a sexy rendezvous with Omar, as he rattled off question after question from the checklist in his head. "Nerves," she thought, as she went on their second date. This time, the lion Omar presented her with was no little beanbag toy, but a good-size stuffed lion that she speculated would not make it home too easily on the train. She pictured herself juggling this lion, her handbag, and a swan full of leftover Atlantic salmon with passion-fruit coulis as she rummaged around for her ticket. Still, the second date was going well, and when he asked her out for a third, she couldn't think of any real reason to say no. She was still smarting from her breakup with Royce, whom she suspected left her for someone else, notwithstanding her lack of evidence. Nevertheless, she needed to move on, and Omar was a nice-enough guy. And just like that, before she even knew what was happening, Quinn was hopelessly entangled with the Clingy Guy. In a matter of months Omar had worked his way into her life in a way that bordered on obsessive. Had she loved him back, it might have been a great beginning to a fabulous relationship. Instead, to Quinn, it felt like Obsess-A-Palooza '06. Quinn would go out with her friends and look around at all the happy couples and resent them terribly. The more she resented them for being happy and actually

ring-ring!

You know you are dating the Clingy Guy when the phone call for a Saturday night date goes like this:

SCENARIO *It's Sunday morning, almost one week before any potential date, and the phone rings.*

him: Hi there you! It's me (*as if, of course, you'll know who "me" is*). I was just watching Martha Stewart and I have some great ideas for us for this week. I downloaded a stain chart so I can do your floors if you want, or you can come shopping with me for an SUV, which we'll need once we start having kids. Unless you want to wait on that. But I wouldn't want to wait too long. You know how pushy my mother can be. Why don't I come over at 6:00 and we'll figure it all out.

you: Okay.

If you were honest with him, here's how your reply would have gone:

you: Who *is* this?

enjoying each other's company, the more she was encouraged to take further advantage of Omar. The final straw was when her best friend strolled in to work one day with a big, fat engagement ring on her finger. In Quinn's mind, this forced her hand. When Omar insisted on a vacation to the rain forests of Costa Rica, which he would no doubt pay for, how could she say no? She had no qualms about letting him take her to the finest hotels, hire a guide to take them through the trails of the rain forest, and buy her a still bigger lion, since there were no real-life lions in Cartago. Quinn used her Clingy Guy for all he was worth, even though she didn't love him and he secretly made her nuts. Sadly, it wasn't even the Clingy Guy's fault that he was driving Quinn batty; everything about relationships made her nuts, and made her really angry, too. She was angry at the way she had been treated in the past, all that she had put up with from former lovers, and angry that she never insisted on more from the men in her life. Now poor, unsuspecting Clingy Guy Omar had to make up for it.

Clingy Guy-isms

With the Clingy Guy, you don't really care if he calls you or not— yet he does, all the time. He'll even phone your friends to get the inside scoop on you: your likes and dislikes, your hopes and dreams, and also what your favorite flower is, so he can show up with five dozen of them on your next date. If you have nothing better to do when he calls, you agree to go out with him. What the heck? It's only a Tuesday and while you hate to be this way, it is also a free dinner. He, on the other hand, is about to go on a real date with

top ten items clingy guy tries
to leave in your apartment

1. Toothbrush
2. Framed photo of himself
3. His insulin (or other lifesaving medication)
4. His wallet
5. His dignity
6. His retainer and night brace
7. A small undetectable video camera
8. His night-vision goggles (oops, didn't mean to leave those)
9. Poems written on your bathroom mirror in lipstick
10. Himself

you, one that he has been thinking about all weekend long. He is nervous, changes his outfit several times, and spends painstakingly long hours on the phone with friends and a Zagat Guide to find the perfect romantic restaurant. You, just looking for some ravioli and a glass of Merlot, show up straight from the gym. He's bought new pants just for this date; you took one of those quickie gym showers and forgot deodorant. The irony here is that your lack of interest in him makes you act so nonplused, he likes you even more. It's a sick cycle that you have created, and good luck getting out of it. Every date, he worries. He worries about everything from the direction of your relationship to how much he should tip the coat-check girl.

You worry, too. You worry that if you go out with him again on a weeknight, this could be the night that Stabler and Benson finally get together and you will be missing the best *Law & Order SVU* episode ever! You may have trouble discerning whether you are actually with the Clingy Guy, or dating a really nice guy that you should decide to take seriously. You may be confused at first, but there are always ways to tell the difference. With a really nice guy who you should take seriously, you'll feel that faint pit-of-stomach rush/butterfly feeling when he kisses you. With the Clingy Guy, it feels like a courtesy kiss.

---

the date-to-sex chart for the clingy guy

Let's say you are on a date with the Clingy Guy and you are not sure what exactly is expected of you afterward. You know he isn't The One, yet his efforts deserve some reward. Here is the system that I recommend:

the date	the score
Hot dog, popcorn, and Heath Ledger movie	*Kiss goodnight while pretending he is Heath Ledger*
Carries your bags around the mall, watches you flirt with bartender	*French kiss*
Guy you really like doesn't call, Clingy Guy takes you out for dinner instead	*Make-out session on the couch*
Clingy Guy helps you move	*Make-out session over the shirt*
Bored on a Saturday night	*Sex*

You don't want to get too close to the Clingy Guy, because it means so much more to him than it does to you. To him a handshake is an extreme gesture—you've touched him!—and if you kiss him, forget it, he's hooked. The worst-case scenario is desperation sex with the Clingy Guy, which will inevitably cause excessive cling. At first you think to yourself, "How much worse could it be?" Just you wait. While you still may be able to recover from this sticky situation, be advised that the Clingy Guy plus sex equals marriage proposal less than two weeks away. Start employing an exit strategy now. Seriously—don't wait! If you have gotten yourself into this predicament, put this book down and get cracking!

Another way to tell if you are indeed with the Clingy Guy is that you feel keenly aware of a few of his annoying little habits—like breathing and walking. But you are in a dating slump and since he thinks you hung the moon, you stick around. At first when you go to the Clingy Guy's apartment you notice that he has a cat, a fact that you find sweet and nurturing. You never dated a guy who had a cat before. "Maybe this means he could be good with children," you think, until you see that he is just as clingy with Fluffy as he is with you. You and Fluffy start to bond over how truly irritating the Clingy Guy can be. Fluffy can sass him and hide under the bed; you are not as lucky. However, when it comes to the Clingy Guy, you, like Fluffy, have the loyalty of a hooker, and either one of you could leave him at a moment's notice. At times, being with the Clingy Guy is a lot like being with one of your girlfriends: although you would never wish a uterus on anyone, it's nice to just talk and shop and pig out together. The Clingy Guy is sensitive enough to be in touch with his feminine side, something that you never before considered in a date. On some days, you think "Aw, he's like my best bud, with a penis," and on others, you feel more like, "UGH, he's like my best bud . . . WITH A PENIS!!" Still, you're sick of that macho crap that other guys have laid on you, and are really ticked off at all of the guys who played games with you. You truly like the break from being treated poorly by guys who aren't worth your time. In light of this, it's a relief that Clingy Guy is so misguidedly devoted. Despite this weird friendship/doormat thing that you're digging, the Clingy Guy is not without fault, and as you get to know him, you will find that the main difference between him and a really nice guy who you should take seriously is that the Clingy Guy has a few very odd quirks, which range from the innocuous to the "get the net" variety.

For example, quirk number one is that for some godforsaken reason, the Clingy Guy hates Ashton Kutcher. Hey, it's America, and he is entitled to love and hate anybody he wants to, but the Clingy Guy hates poor Ashton so much that he keeps a file on him. It's an actual file in a hanging file folder that he displays proudly next to his computer. The Clingy Guy collects every article, every tabloid piece, and every story he can find in which Ashton is made to look silly. You don't know why he does this, but you can venture a guess: Ashton is a hunk and a half, who the Clingy Guy simultaneously despises and aspires to emulate. It's an odd sort of envy/hate/obsession male thing that you don't quite understand. The Clingy Guy is also the type of guy who has a special outfit that he cooks in: splattering oil ruined his shirt once while he was making eggplant parmesan. He was never able to get the stain out, so he will not take *that* risk again.

In Doreen's case, her Clingy Guy's quirk was carried over from his last relationship. He had what he called his "hobby," which entailed recording *The Price Is Right* and watching it with Doreen every night during dinner. Doreen's Clingy Guy had just gotten out of a marriage, and used to do this very thing with his ex-wife. Doreen didn't know why watching *The Price Is Right* together every night constituted "fun couple activity" for them, and found the fact that he wanted to incorporate it into his new romance with her quite strange. For Doreen, her Clingy Guy was never a boyfriend

·· in a nutshell ·····

the fantasy The Clingy Guy will suddenly grow a backbone and demand some respect from you, his boss, his mother, and all the women who have wronged him, and then your relationship will finally be on equal footing and fabulous.

the harsh reality Once he finally does grow a backbone, you will be one of the women he will tell off and feel thankful that he didn't end up with.

how you broke up You never really broke up with the Clingy Guy, did you? You just waited him out. Either he found someone else to obsess over or you changed your cell phone number.

but instead, an immediate husband. One day she was meeting him for a first date over a dry martini; the next minute she had an insta-hubby. He began by sending her not one but five dozen roses after their first date. When she arrived home from work, she found her doorman waiting outside to console her, as he was sure that an amount of flowers that large must mean a death in the family. "Not yet," she assured him. The Clingy Guy has many other little peculiarities, too many to enumerate, but suffice it to say they will involve seemingly innocuous things like peanut butter, light bulbs, and a weird thing he does with his mouth. And inevitably there will be one major quirk; you know which one I'm talking about. This quirk is the special, unique-to-your-own-Clingy-Guy trait that you pretend not to notice because you know that when you do, you will, once and for all, be done with him.

The Clingy Guy's most maddening quirk, the one that will eventually sink him, is that, since day one, he has subtly done everything you have asked of him. He has completely submersed himself in the service of your every desire, at the expense of himself. This is typical Clingy Guy behavior. You mention that you don't care for his friend Markus: boom, he doesn't see him anymore. You tell him that his ceiling is peeling: boom, painters are coming next weekend. Little by little you start to notice that almost every little comment that you make about the Clingy Guy's wardrobe, friendships, and life have now become his raison d'être. At this point, not only is Clingy Guy grating on your last nerve; you begin to see that he is willing to completely give up who he is just to please you.

In Quinn's case, she justified her relationship with Omar in ways that were completely unfair to him, as if he were put on this earth to serve her and repent for the sins of all the bad men she had dated before him. This was bad behavior on Quinn's part, but at the same time, true to his Clingy Guy ways, Omar did allow her to walk all over him. Quinn eventually let Omar go, because she knew that some other woman out there may appreciate him more. But what about you? Why did you date your Clingy Guy? The reasons are as individual as you are. Was it a simple rebound from a guy who wasn't fair to you? Or are you a bossy sort of gal, who likes her men to be half-man, half-doormat? By the time you are ready to break up with the Clingy Guy, he has worked your nerves so much that, while you would still help him out if he were trapped under something heavy, you can barely consider dating him. You begin to see that what started out as an ego boost for you or a small diversion on your way to Mr. Right has now become a grim predicament.

Saddled with the Clingy Guy, you now see how maybe you, in the not-so-distant past, gave *your* heart too easily to someone who wasn't that interested. You start to see yourself in the Clingy Guy, and you respect him even less. Doesn't he see that it's hopeless for him? Someone should say something to him, and while we're at it, why didn't someone say something to you when you were in your last relationship wasting your time? Aha! the Clingy Guy finally makes sense, the poor fool. He is there for you to learn a lesson from and not for you to spend the rest of your life with. (Heavens no!) You don't have time to fix the Clingy Guy, since his desperation is overshadowed by his eccentricities. Even if you stay with him a little longer out of pity, you will want to push him out of a moving vehicle very soon.

Why You Dated the Clingy Guy in the First Place

When you first met the Clingy Guy you knew that you weren't that interested in him, but you were seriously sick of the games you'd been playing with the men you were actually interested in. You were happy to have an opportunity to finally date someone who was never going to play a game with you, and though you hate to cop to this, it was nice to be with someone you could control. You were coming off of several crappy dates and maybe even another broken heart, and you were done! The Clingy Guy was your chance to be the heartbreaker this time, as well as your chance to just be treated like the queen that you are. You may lose your patience with the Clingy Guy, but you also really liked the attention he showered you with. "Now that's more like it," you thought. You were not thinking about your future at that point, so much as you were thinking about your past. You were thinking about how you had

if the clingy guy went to a shrink
she would tell him . . .

That he probably has Dependent Personality Disorder. Duh! Like you needed a shrink to tell you that he is dependent and it's a problem. The shrink has the same issues with him. The Clingy Guy will not leave after his fifty minutes are up. The Clingy Guy will stick around to see if the shrink needs a lift home or will try to have a drink with her after work. The Clingy Guy knows no boundaries! These are the symptoms of Dependent Personality Disorder:

- *He has difficulty making everyday decisions without advice:* When his mother said, "If Jimmy jumped off the Brooklyn Bridge, would you do it too?" he replied, "Did Jimmy call?"
- *Difficulty saying no to others or disagreeing with others:* To fit in, he stole gum when he was five years old, beer as a teenager, and did insider trading just so the guys at his club would golf with him.
- *He can't initiate projects on his own (due to lack of self-confidence):* Without a girlfriend egging him on, the Clingy Guy will forever live in a half-painted, half-furnished rental, full of unpacked boxes.
- *He is unable to care for himself. Like any good boy he washes behind his ears. Sadly, that's where the washing ends.*
- *He urgently needs to be in another relationship when one ends:* After getting dumped in the restaurant, the Clingy Guy starts at the waitress, heads toward the big-breasted bartender, and when the coat-check girl rejects him too, his desperation makes Alfred the busboy a little nervous.

been treated and what you had settled for in previous relationships that you most certainly should not have put up with, stuff that you may actually still be angry about. With the Clingy Guy, it doesn't even occur to you that maybe it's wrong to date someone you really aren't that into. You are sick of being alone on a Friday night, damn it! And you do have your cousin's wedding coming up in March. The Clingy Guy will totally drive you to the wedding, which is 500 miles away, and he will even buy a new suit for the event. His hopes will be raised, then dashed giving him hope-lash.

A Part of You Knows Better, But . . .

You date the Clingy Guy while you are experiencing "dating entitlement," the irrational notion you have that says, "The dating Gods *owe* me." Nevertheless, when you get home from being out with the Clingy Guy, assuming that you just could not bear his company anymore and told him not to sleep over, you still feel lonely. You notice that you feel more empty after spending time with the wrong person than you do after spending the entire evening alone. Being single for a while and not dating anyone at all should have been an opportunity for you to decide what you really want from your future (and to hack away at your Essentials List, of course). Instead you filled the silence with the Clingy Guy, and where did that get you? The exact same place—alone! But this time, being alone would have been the better option, because now you've gone and hurt somebody else in the process. You have left devastation in your wake, and you feel like a hurricane date-monster, left with a side of guilt to go with that helping of humility you now feel.

By now the Clingy Guy is so totally in love with you that you forget to see him as a person, and his little oddities don't help his situation. He seems more like a cartoon character than a man with real feelings that you should be concerned about. How could you be? He's asphyxiating you with his incessant phone calls and unwarranted attention! And the more he can sense that he's irritating you with his habits, the more he tries to take your mental and emotional pulse every five minutes, asking "Now what are you thinking?" "Now what?" At this point, it's all you can do not to scream "SHUT UP AND GOODBYE."

 *your jewel of wisdom*

It's not like you went into this thinking he was a diamond or anything. You knew that what you had here was a cubic zirconium. It was a pretty good replica, just so long as nobody got too close or looked too hard, and it was better than going bare, especially to a party. The cubic zirconium may not be valuable, but the lessons you learned here with the Clingy Guy certainly were. Since you are so smart you knew all of this already, so the question you should ask yourself is, why were you avoiding real intimacy by dating him? Why did you continue when it was painfully obvious that he wasn't The One? What was it you were trying to avoid? At least this is an opportunity to learn more about yourself and what would be of the most value on your Essentials List, so all's well that ends well, I guess.

PART THREE

the uneducated

i go for two kinds of men. the kind with muscles, and the kind without.

—mae west

This section of guys finds you in the throes of mindless masculinity. Suffice it to say that some are motivated by an overabundance of testosterone, while others, an overabundance of Bud Light. The beneficial aspects of dating the uneducated are primal and almost prehistoric; you finally understand what it may have been like to hunt for bear and run with the wild dogs. These are the men with whom you do not seek knowledge, so much as a diversion from the endless search for Mr. Right. You fancy a shag and they are eager to please regardless of the fact that there is a time limit on this relationship, i.e., how long you can stay with them and still maintain your sanity level.

chapter seven

the younger guy

personality profile

The Younger Guy tends to talk about the same things over and over and over. He is simple if not consistent. Because he grew up with technology, he enjoys jokes that revolve around Microsoft, pictures that put the president's head on a gorilla's body, and any Web site that has to do with bands, beer, or boobs. He reads blogs about Xbox 360 or PlayStation 3, and if a device has a controller (called a joystick in your day), the Younger Guy is on it! His favorite book is *The Moron's Guide to Napping*, and your first date will be an afternoon at the zoo followed by pizza. Caution: he is still finding himself, so conversations may be an unnecessarily deep glimpse into nothing in particular. But afterward he will feel very connected to you.

The ultimate "screw you" to your smug, married girlfriends

The Younger Guy will date for food, lodging, sex, whatever he can scam. At best, he is fun for your friends to flirt with on those nights when there is nobody around; at worst, he drains your bank account. He may also be called "the Starving Artist," but he isn't terribly good at his art, either. "The fact that nobody understands him does not make him an artist," you think to yourself; but you do not mention this, for fear of ruining his still-developing self-esteem. The best part about the Younger Guy is that he brings back memories of summer crushes . . . from when you were twelve. Just be warned that the Younger Guy will take a nap ten minutes after he's been awake—after all, the young ones need their sleep; they're still growing! Have a sleeve of Oreo cookies on you at all times, so as to avoid unnecessary crankiness when he wakes up, and you'll be a hit with the Younger Guy! The Younger Guy may be pursuing some kind of creative endeavor, such as writing the great American novel, waiting to sign his record deal with Sony, or anticipating his inevitable meeting with Spielberg. These lofty aspirations of his are a sort of modern version of wanting to be a fireman or an astronaut. Just be prepared: he will probably ask you to come see his play, art exhibit, Mummenchanz reenactment, whatever his "art" is this month. Because sitting in the audience among his young friends makes you feel like a mother seeing her little boy in a school play, you may want to consider just supporting him from afar.

"Supporting" the Younger Guy usually entails paying for dinner. At first it may be cute that he can only afford Taco Loco

(Taco Bell was just a dream to him) but after a while you'll start to long for a real meal served on a real plate with a cloth napkin instead of ramen noodles on Dixie plates with a Bounty. When he invites you over for a late-night snack consisting of Twinkies and pot, you may begin to second-guess your dating choices.

The Younger Guy always knows the cool new places to go hang out, and that would be great if he didn't keep calling you "dude." He is a blast to date—until he asks you for a dollar and

a history of dating
interracial marriages

1967 brought the aptly named "Loving Decision." This was the case that overturned the laws against interracial marriage. Here's the story: Two residents of Virginia—Mildred Jeter, an African-American woman, and Richard Loving, a white man— were married in the District of Columbia in June of 1958. Shortly after their marriage, the Lovings returned to their home state of Virginia and established their marital abode in Caroline County. In October 1958 a grand jury issued an indictment charging the Lovings with violating Virginia's ban on interracial marriages. The Lovings pleaded guilty to the charge and were sentenced to one year in jail. They appealed to the Supreme Court, which found that the Fourteenth Amendment of our Constitution had been violated. It clearly states that the freedom to marry, or not marry, a person of another race cannot be infringed upon by the state. Because of this decision, sixteen other states changed their laws regarding interracial marriages.

starts chasing down the ice-cream truck with absolutely no sense of irony. You take solace in the fact that it is true what they say about the energy of the Younger Guy; he *can* go all night. Everyone knows that women reach their sexual peak at 36, and guys reach theirs at 19, so mathematically, this relationship works perfectly. At first, you even think that he is being adventurous

⋯ ring-ring! ⋯⋯⋯⋯⋯⋯⋯⋯

You know you are dating the Younger Guy when the phone call for a Saturday night date goes like this:

SCENARIO *It's Saturday Night, the phone rings.*

you: Hello?

him: (*In a muffled disguised voice*) Hi can I speak to Mike Hunt? Is Mike Hunt there?

you: I know it's you.

him: (*Still in a muffled disguised voice with giggling in the background*) I'm looking for Amanda Huginkiss.

you: Younger Guy, stop it, I know it's you.

him: (*Still not giving it up*) Is your refrigerator running?

you: I still know it's you . . . c'mon, what do you want?

him: Okay you got me . . . I was calling because I was wonder— . . . ooh, I have call waiting, hang on . . . (he never comes back)

If you were honest with him, here's how that conversation should have gone:

him: Do you have Prince Albert in a can . . .

you: Wrong Number.

for having sex in the back of his Geo until you find out that it's because he still lives at home with his mother and that the car is hers. He does have that fun young spirit, and his generation has brought back that free-love thing again. No commitments here, just a zipless indiscriminate screw, a handful of Mike and Ikes and he's off.

God knows that he fills you with a newfound sexual freedom. You also realize that being with the Younger Guy gives you the chance to make up for all of those years of saying, "I wish I knew then what I know now," because he is like a dating do-over. With the Younger Guy you get to erase all the mistakes that you made with guys his age when *you* were that age, and you get to try again.

Younger Guy-isms

When you hook up with the Younger Guy, you feel empowered and rebellious. Dating someone so much younger than you breaks all convention, and is a really good "screw you" to all of your self-righteous, smug, married girlfriends who didn't think you could land a man. Take Gabrielle, for example, who met her Younger Guy, Bay (short for Baylor) at a concert in the park over the summer. Bay was taking a year off from Harvard. He was about to be a senior and his wrestling coach thought that if he wanted to be an Olympic wrestler, he needed an intensive year of training before returning to school, so he moved home for the year in order to train. Gabrielle knew that Bay was going to be going back to school at some point, so in her mind, her romance with him was never going to be long-term. In fact, she didn't even expect it to last until the end of the summer. She loved to go out with her friends and when one of them would tell her, "I met this great guy, he's a CEO," she would reply, "Oh, that's nothing, my boyfriend is the captain of the wrestling team." It was a laugh they could all share. Just the silliness of the thought that someone her age could be with someone who *really was* the captain of his wrestling team was hilarious.

With the Younger Guy, part of his charm is that he doesn't have to follow all the conventions of real life, real careers, and real dates. Sure, he may call you on Saturday morning for a Saturday-night date, but if you're into it, no problem! And if you can put up with his never-ending poo jokes and butt humor, you will definitely have a good time.

The drawbacks to dating the Younger Guy become apparent when you meet his parents, and realize that you have the same 1984 Van Halen concert T-shirt that he found in his mother's drawer (obviously a covetable fashion item, but does he *have* to keep calling it *vintage*?). Unfortunately, poor Younger Guy doesn't know good music—he only knows boy bands—and while you have light bulbs whose careers have lasted longer, you try your best to educate him. Sadly, in the end you find that the musical generation gap is just too big. To you The Police were cool; to him Sting is just a fifty-year-old weirdo who does yoga. You saw Henry Rollins at CBGB's with Black Flag; he saw Henry Rollins reviewing films and reciting poetry on IFC. You remember the controversy when Ice-T released "Cop Killer," he remembers the controversy when Ice-T almost didn't renew his contract with *Law & Order*. To you "Old School" means Afrika Bambaataa, Run-D.M.C., and

·· in a nutshell ···········

the fantasy The Younger Guy will turn to you one day and say, "Darling, do you want crème fraîche with your caviar?"

the harsh reality The Younger Guy will turn to you and say, "Dude, do you want fries with that?"

how you broke up You called his mom and told her to come pick him up.

the Sugarhill Gang; to him it means Will Ferrell running around naked and screaming at Vince Vaughn. It's funny and laughable at first, but eventually, it starts to feel funny-sad.

In the end, the Younger Guy is best when used for anecdotes while sitting around with your girls and bemoaning the temperamental male ego. After all, he hasn't developed one yet. He is for humor purposes only and should not be taken seriously. Date him at your peril.

Why You Dated the Younger Guy in the First Place

Very few of us go out looking for *much* younger men to date. You may encounter dating prospects who are younger by a few years, perhaps, but nobody goes out looking for someone to hang out with who will make them *feel* old. There are enough wrinkle-cream ads and teenage pop stars saturating the media for that. Your relationship with the Younger Guy may come about in a variety of ways. Perhaps you mistook him for being older than he is when you first met him, or maybe you *kind of* knew that he was younger, but thought when you met him that if anything happened between the two of you, it would just be a one-night stand. In any case, the Younger Guy interested you because he still has that "conquer the world" thing going on, and you found it intoxicating. His ideals and naiveté, combined with his good looks and willingness to look at you as an all-knowing goddess, made a relationship with him irresistible.

Stuff that you've done a million times—like air travel, ordering off the adult menu, and going to the aquarium without a permission slip—are new and exciting to him. You are in control in a way that you never were before. It isn't like it was with the Hot Guy (who was fascinated by sock puppets), or the Clingy Guy (who was your punching bag). The Younger Guy sees you as his ideal woman. After all, he may be younger than you, but he isn't crazy! You finally have the chance to be treated right, albeit ten years too late. The Younger Guy has the potential to be molded by you. He's got that new-guy smell.

A Part of You Knows Better, But . . .

You finally have the opportunity to build your own man out of this willing lump of boy clay. He hasn't fully developed yet, so what's so wrong with helping him along in a better direction, really? Don't you owe it to all of womankind to leave men better than you found them? In the meantime, you harbor thoughts of turning the Younger Guy into the best boyfriend you've ever had. You've heard stories of women with husbands at least twelve years younger, and they're very happy! But while this urban legend *could be* true, it's not likely, at least not for you, and not right now.

You didn't start dating the Younger Guy because you wanted to be happy and thought he could make you happy; you started dating the Younger Guy when you thought you just might like to have sex with no attachments. You started dating him because you never thought you would want to get serious with him. Gabrielle, for example, knew for a fact that she didn't want to settle down, and was a perfect candidate for a Younger Guy relationship. Gabrielle was from a family filled with divorces. Her parents were divorced, her aunts and uncles had all gotten divorces, and she really didn't know any happy marriages. As a result, she decided early on that she didn't want to be married. She liked the idea of dating, enjoying lots of different kinds of men, and not having to commit to anyone in particular. She didn't want children, she knew that, so there was no reason to be married, no reason to settle down, and no reason to shy away from her transient Younger Guy. But Gabrielle's relationship with Bay just

signs that your date with younger guy
·· is not going well ············

- ◆ Whenever you start a story he says "Break it down, sister."
- ◆ Toward the end of dinner he says, "I have to eat dessert fast, my parents will be coming for me soon."
- ◆ When you ask where he is working he says proudly, "Not only am I working at McDonald's, but I had to pull some strings to get the job there."

went on and on, until one day she realized that an entire year had passed and pretty soon, Bay was going to be getting back to Boston. In the blink of an eye lots of time had passed, and her "nothing serious" relationship had been going on for longer than she had planned.

So what happened in your own Younger Guy relationship? Here's one scenario: Somewhere between "he's just a one-night stand" and the epiphany that you've been with your Younger Guy for longer than you should have, you actually started to think that maybe this Younger Guy thing could be something real, even though that isn't how you intended things to be in the first place. Sure, he was clear that he would be a) going back to school, b) thinking about moving to another city, or c) never wanting to get married. But somewhere between here and there, you made

ten items in the younger guy's apartment
that cost less than $1.99

1. His bed
2. His couch
3. His favorite sweater
4. His lunch box for school
5. His sneakers
6. His 'Best of Lisa Loeb' CD
7. A six-pack of generic beer
8. Mystery canned fruit and/or vegetables in his cupboard
9. 12-pack of TP
10. His soap on a rope

the mistake of thinking that just because the Younger Guy was younger, he would be your puppy dog and would follow you wherever you decided the relationship should go. In reality, you really didn't respect the Younger Guy, or take him seriously. He was never someone who you wanted a real *relationship* with, but now that you have one, you've become completely attached to him, despite the fact that you knew better. The more comfortable you got, the more uncomfortable he got. Your generational differences were fine at first, but eventually his buddy's jokes that you went to high school with his mother started to bug him. It is no longer funny when his friends call you his "old lady" and now the Younger Guy wants out. Suddenly, you find yourself on the business end of an "I'm just not ready for anything this serious" conversation.

Perhaps, like Gabrielle, you were the heartbreaker in your Younger Guy scenario. He was falling hard for you all of these months, and you just liked having an admirer. Deep down inside, a part of you was thinking, "Who cares how you feel about him? You've got your very own fan club!" Finally the day came when you had to let him down gently, because you'd met an adult that you wanted to date. It was nice for a while having the Younger Guy gaze up at you like a child gazing up at a clown doing magic at a birthday party. You loved the attention, you loved feeling smarter, and you certainly loved that he had stamina for lots of stuff. You just never loved him, and now you've gone and broken a perfectly sweet guy's heart.

In Gabrielle's case, about two weeks before Bay returned to college in Boston, he told Gabrielle that he wanted her to come up and visit him as much as she could, that he wanted to try to continue their relationship long distance, and that he really felt

she would tell him . . .

His generation has so many weird things going on anyway. You've experienced the Younger Guy's sexual proclivity for ideas that your generation only heard about or read about on porn sites. A shrink who saw Younger Guy in her office might say that he is from a generation that is sexually permissive, one in which everyone grew up on Ritalin, and that the combination of attention span difficulties and sexual appetite may have caused the Younger Guy to experience life in fast forward. Maybe your Younger Guy is at this extreme. Maybe he is a total fetishist and while we're at it, let's explore his hyperactivity/ADD too. Hey, it could happen. If he has a fetishism thing going on it would look like this:

◆ *He has recurrent and intense sexual arousal from fantasies or behaviors involving the use of non-living objects:* So, when you came home and found the Younger Guy wearing your feminine undergarments as a joke, he may not have been entirely joking. Just like the time when he insisted on trying on your spike heels, claiming he was coming up with a Halloween costume. It's not Halloween, honey, it's April Fools' Day, and you are it!

◆ *Fantasies rule him; he wants to enact them all the time:* He will even leave a class or skip work for a day to hang out if you are willing. His priorities are sex, him, sex with him, and candy.

◆ *Fetish objects are not limited to female clothing, you lucky thing, you!* He could also be into food items, stuffed animals . . . who knows, maybe even a vibrator? That wouldn't be *so* bad, now, would it?

If he has hyperactivity or ADD, it will look more like this:

◆ *He fails to give close attention to detail:* Note to self—In the heat of passion, watch out! You have no idea where he is gonna stick that thing! And if he calls out the wrong name, try not to be insulted; he just can't be bothered with details!

◆ *He has difficulty sustaining attention on task:* So, you are no longer surprised when, in the middle of sex, he gets up and makes a sandwich. If you're hungry, too, keep dreaming, because he certainly won't remember to make one for you.

◆ *He doesn't listen when spoken to directly:* "Sweetie, turn off the light in the bathroom . . . Sweetie, turn off the light in the bathroom . . . Sweetie, turn off the light in the bathroom . . . Never mind, I'll get it."

◆ *He doesn't follow through on instructions:* He stops at Lather, never makes it to Rinse. Forget about Repeat.

◆ *He avoids tasks requiring sustained mental effort:* Which explains why his generation abbreviates everything. By the time they get to the end of the sentence they forgot their point.

◆ *He loses stuff—a lot:* He lost his wallet while trying to find his car keys, which he couldn't see because he locked his glasses in the car.

◆ *He is easily distracted:* He enjoys games like "Look at the shiny metal object!"

they could make it work. Gabrielle was shocked! "What am I going to do, go up to his dorm room and hang out with all his friends at the Hasty Pudding Club?" she thought. "What am I, twenty?" All along Gabrielle thought that her relationship with Bay was just a fun sex thing that just went on a little too long; she never took him seriously on any level. Now she could see that she was about to hurt him.

Gabrielle, like most Younger Guy daters, never admitted to herself that Bay was just a diversion. She never thought he was anything more than a playmate—but when she told him goodbye, she recognized that it meant more to him. At first she thought, "Oh, he was really into me, that is so cute!" but when she saw how hurt he really was, she felt terrible. She knew that, in the future, she should try to find a happy medium. Maybe she could date guys who were just a little bit younger than she was, guys she still respected, and that maybe having *some* consequence to her actions in a relationship, rather than absolutely none, would be more fun and fulfilling for her in the long run.

your jewel of wisdom

The Younger Guy is less of a jewel and more like one of those beaded necklaces from high school that came apart, but you left it in your jewelry box drawer hoping to one day restring it. Let it go. The lesson here is that any guy who is wrong for you is just clutter in your life and doesn't serve you in any way. Be selfish in this respect. Take the lesson and move along—there is nothing more to see here.

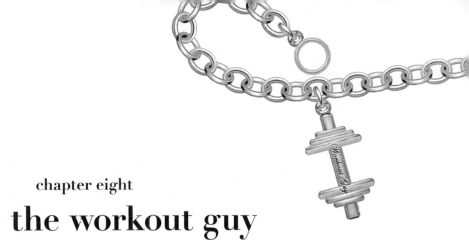

chapter eight
the workout guy

personality profile

You are at a party and some guy turns to you, points to your chocolate appletini and your Marlboro Light and says, "You know, that isn't very good for you." He's cute enough so you don't give him your usual response of "I don't know what your problem is but I bet it's hard to pronounce." Instead you are intrigued that the Workout Guy has taken an interest in you. He seems genuinely concerned with your well-being. You don't see it as the self-righteousness that it is and freely give him your cell phone number, curious about entering the "culture of the bods" to which he so obviously belongs. Just beware; his personality is bi—and tri—dimensional: biceps and triceps, that is.

He'll never be as into you as he is into himself

The Workout Guy is the guy you met at the gym, or while jogging at the local high school track, or maybe he roller bladed into you at a stoplight. Either way, he's cute and seems datable—at first. But he'll never be as into you as he is into himself. Whether he's flexing in the mirror or having endless discussions about physical accomplishments (you can be sure he means how much he can bench press, and not how good he is in the sack), he's just another stepping stone on your way to finding The One. Not only is he dull as dirt once taken out of the workout environment, but his giant ego leads him to assume he is the only man in your life before you really even have a relationship going. He'll call and say, "Hi, it's me" when you've only just started dating. At first glance his minor arrogance comes off as extreme confidence, until you realize that it is masking some *major* insecurities—the kind that will take a crowbar and several bottles of Valium to fix.

He is the guy who may seem redeemable for valuable romantic prizes, but don't be fooled! He is too damaged even for supergirl-friend. Besides, if you're going to work that hard for something, shouldn't it be for your own fetching abs? The Workout Guy is really into nutrition, and while that side of him can be a good thing, he sacrifices fun for discipline. Nobody that highly disciplined should even be allowed to date! One of the best things about dating in general are those whimsical little surprises, those moments of unpredictability that lead to wondrous romance, all of which are lost on the Workout Guy. The most unpredictable thing about the Workout Guy is that he just switched from the

a history of dating

⋅⋅⋅ the media and the single girl ⋅⋅⋅⋅⋅

Women's ability to choose the men they would date was reflected in the pop culture of the 1970s. Shows like *The Dating Game*, in which a woman asked questions of three bachelors and chose the one that she fancied most, were a reflection of what was happening in society. Other shows, including *Mary Tyler Moore*, *That Girl*, and *Rhoda*, portrayed women as strong and independent and men as just accessories to them. During this time it became okay to be career-focused and have men come second on your list of priorities. This was a far cry from just a few decades earlier, when a woman was just another of her man's possessions.

regular yellow Gatorade to that fancy, neon blue one, which he likes because it makes him pee funny colors. When he takes you out for dinner, he calculates the carb-to-protein ratio on everything you eat, and you can forget about dessert, let alone any sexual dalliances involving whipped cream! The Workout Guy doesn't eat sweets. That's years and years of chocolate and Häagen-Dazs that he'll never get back. You have to understand this: You are dating a sizable and muscular male version of a thirteen-year-old girl with an eating disorder.

Workout Guy-isms

Despite all of the Workout Guy's freakishly disciplined little rules, he is hunky and strong and you feel petite and protected

⋯ ring-ring! ⋯

You know you are dating the Workout Guy when the phone call for a Saturday night date goes like this:

SCENARIO *It's Monday evening; he's got to plan out the week. The phone rings.*

him: *(panting)* Hey. Sorry I'm a little out of breath. I was just giving my lats one last blast. I love feelin' the burn.

you: Yeah, that's great.

him: Whooo, so . . . ah . . . Saturday night? I'm training late, so if you want to meet for a wheat grass I can do it around nine.

you: Ummm . . . okay. Do you want to grab dinner? There's a new Indian restaurant in my neighborhood that I wanted to try.

him: Indian food??!!! It's just not worth the extra calories; it's just not worth it!

you: Okay, I guess I'll see you at nine at the juice bar then.

If you were honest with him, here's how the conversation should have gone:

him: You want to meet for a wheat grass after my workout Saturday night?

you: Listen you muscle-headed bitch-titted circus freak! It is Saturday night and neither one of us is getting any younger! So either you take me out to a decent restaurant and stop feeding me braised chicken and rice served in Tupperware, or I will tell everyone at the gym that you cried like a baby at the end of *Pumping Iron*!

when you are with him no matter what size you are. Plus, his massive ego is such that he has you convinced that, because he has chosen you, you must be *some* prize—which, of course, you are. The Workout Guy is superficial, and for a while that's okay with you. You are sick of trying to "connect" with a guy, and the Workout Guy is your chance to just *be*. It's relaxing being with him because there isn't much to him. You can hang out a "gone fishin'" sign, and not care about where the relationship is going, or who feels what about whom. You may even get a little of the Workout Guy's crazy disciplined lifestyle to rub off on you. Hell, maybe while dating him you'll get in the best shape of your life—free! You just have to put up with his peculiar personality and the fact that sometimes when you look at him he reminds you of an orangutan.

Heather was just out of a two-year relationship. The last few months of it were particularly hard and she just needed a break. She pressed the dating hold button, and started to work on herself from both the inside and out; but first, the out. So, when her new kickboxing class instructor, Curtis, asked if anyone was looking for a personal trainer, she thought this would be perfect for her. By the tenth session she had a little crush on Curtis, and asked him out for coffee. He gave her a thirty-minute lecture on why caffeine was not good for the body, and what constricted blood cells look like, but then agreed to go if she found a place that had an organic juice bar. She was a bit turned off that he was so high-maintenance . . . but his buns of steel ruled out.

The Workout Guy has pet peeves too. He hates the fitness craze and all the diet books for a number of reasons. One, he doesn't understand the lack of discipline that allows people to get so fat and out of shape in the first place, and he sees the glut of fitness gurus as exploitation of Big Mac lovers. That's the Workout Guy's conundrum: he, too, needs there to be Big Mac lovers; he needs people to feel superior to (and to train; how else is he supposed to keep himself in bulk powder?). "Let them be fat and happy while he is fit and healthy," he thinks. As far as he's concerned, it's evolutionary. The Workout Guy swears by Darwin's Survival of the Fittest theory. He has it embroidered on pillows. It is his mantra, and he is highly competitive. He's even competitive with you. You have heard him say to people, "I beat Kyla at racquetball four times in a row" (assuming your name is Kyla) and you don't know why you care, but you do. You'll show him.

The Workout Guy lives by the "no sex before a competition" motto, which also extends to business meetings, PowerPoint presentations, and Thanksgiving dinner at his parents' house. You enjoy the cynical, egomaniacal side of him; it not only amuses you, but also secretly gives you a slight boost of superiority. His cynicism makes him angry about many things: he hates steroids in baseball (he considers those guys wusses), he hates skinny fashion models, and he truly resents all those movie stars who are now bulking up. To him they have all taken his sport away. He is angry that Demi Moore and Matthew McConaughey took up weight training, and it just makes him crazy that his quiet gym is now flooded with non-workout people, all working in solidarity to have arms like Madonna's. Worst of all he hates the New Year's resolution people, because they crowd his gym from December to February. Good girlfriend that you are, you remind him that he can take solace in the fact that, by March, he'll have his haven back.

Together you and the Workout Guy laugh at all the newbies at the gym, with their "Oooh, I was so sore today!" and "Oh, it's worse two days later, just you wait!" banter. You join him in feeling condescending and arrogant (never mind the fact that you just joined the gym yourself). After all of those years you spent on the losing color-war team at camp, or the worst afterschool softball league team in history, you are at last one of the cool athletic kids.

The Workout Guy measures life in reps and hours. He is more excited about his powerlifting week than he is about your three-month anniversary together. The Workout Guy will talk during sex, but don't dare talk to him between sets—he's concentrating! He uses phrases like "bulking phase" when asking for a raise at work, and when he travels he makes sure the hotel has a gym (though he will most certainly bemoan how lousy it is.) Let's face

·· in a nutshell ··

the fantasy The Workout Guy is useful around the house. He will lift every box, repair every leaky faucet, and open every jar. He makes a great last-minute moving man and is ready and willing to pose for a charity calendar or at least audition for *Playgirl*.

the harsh reality Though he is excited to see you, that is in fact a banana in his pocket.

how you broke up A horrible mishap! While you were jogging with him one afternoon the olive fell out of your martini glass, and you knew it was time to call it quits (with him—never with drinking!).

it: you are dating an anatomy chart. He has posters on his apartment walls that read, "lift heavy or go home" and "pump till you puke."

While you realize that the Workout Guy doesn't mean a lot in your life and that he is a simple conundrum of nil and zilch, you are also aware that your ass has never looked better. That's the thing to remember when you've glommed on to the Workout Guy: as soon as you are in your skinny jeans, it is time for the termi-date. You feel muscle-y and strong; you are the Termi-dater (sorry, couldn't pass that one up). But alas, it is the end, finito, and thanks for the nutrition bars.

ten items you can't lift or figure out how to use
in workout guy's apartment

1. His supplement schedule
2. His jockstrap
3. His testicles
4. The weight bench next to his bed
5. The weight bench in the kitchen
6. The weight bench in the bathtub
7. That weird contraption he asked you not to touch that you thought was a sex toy
8. Light switches (could be for the tanning bed, could be for the lamp, not really sure)
9. His vat of protein powder, which you thought was Coffee-Mate
10. The dead hooker he killed during a weekend of 'roid rage

Why You Dated the Workout Guy in the First Place

Face it: You liked being a trophy for a guy who is obsessed with trophies. He has a case full from his younger days, and maybe he still competes in athletics now. You are another possession for a superficial egomaniac who deems you are worthy of him. You dated him because your ego was shot and you were sick of having to do self-esteem-building things like finding new ways to feel good about yourself on the inside. He had a huge ego; maybe he could just give you a little piece of it. It's not like he would miss it anyway. Yes, you care about world peace and starvation, but you want to look good as well and you have spent money on your hair and your wardrobe and you want to be recognized for being cute and adorable for once and not just smart and sensible. It's the American way. If you don't think so, look at the amount of money thirty-somethings spend on plastic surgery versus how much they spend on adult education. You are concerned with what you look like, and this is your time to revel in that. Get your nails done twice a week, and your hair highlighted, and buy new workout clothes—you are entitled to not have to look deeper for once in your godforsaken life. Just remember that no matter how much you indulge that side of you, you will never rival his level of shallowness, but you damn sure will try.

Look, you have asked about your derriére in many a pair of jeans, and whether certain shoes go with a certain bag, and whether your mascara is running, so this isn't really new to you. We're women—it's what we do in the privacy of our own little group. So what? It's high time you were appreciated for what you were on the outside for a change; you spent a lot of money. It

The shrink would say that it's one thing to be interested in exercise—she may even stress the importance of physical fitness to the Workout Guy's health and longevity—but the Workout Guy's extreme behavior puts him in a whole *other* category. Your Workout Guy could have a garden-variety case of Obsessive Compulsive Disorder (OCD). You may have heard this term many times before, but what you may not know is the range of OCD, which can be anything from obsessively washing your hands to checking 150 times to make sure you've turned off the lights before leaving the house. It can also be extreme hoarding behavior, or saving stuff—and not in the pack-rat way either. Since this isn't one of *those* books, let's not completely gross you out, but suffice it to say that the things extreme OCD people hoard are items that most of us would get rid of immediately, say by flushing. Anyway, the Workout Guy doesn't have anything that drastic. But he does have a form of OCD, more O than C in this case. Here's how to tell:

◆ *He is preoccupied with details, lists, organizing, and schedules, to such a degree that the reason behind the activity itself is lost:* At first you thought it was kinky that he had a sex list he liked you to follow—"kiss here, lick there"—till you realized that it was no different than his workout routine. Ten reps of fondling, ten reps of biceps curls, same thing.

- *He exhibits extreme perfectionism:* You have to wonder about a guy who has more beauty rituals than Ivana Trump and complains that the dry cleaners don't do a good enough job. I mean, c'mon.
- *He is excessively devoted to his "thing," at the exclusion of other leisure activities:* This includes seeing a movie or anything else that you ask him to do at normal times. If he's at the gym, you are flying solo, no questions asked—and he is *usually* at the gym.
- *He is overconscientious and scrupulously inflexible:* To him, the phrase "my way or the highway" is no joke. He has it in needlepoint.
- *He is unable to discard stuff:* See the previous information about hoarding things. Let's not go there.
- *He is reluctant to delegate tasks to others unless you do it* exactly *the way the Workout Guy wants you to:* EXACTLY. Did you hear me? I said DO IT LIKE THIS . . . oh crap, move aside, let me!
- Overall, he is just rigid and stubborn.

doesn't mean that you are not a kind and caring individual. The Workout Guy gives you the chance to open up that superficial side of you that just wants to self-righteously scream out, "Nice load, buttzilla" to some woman at the food court who made an unfortunate choice when she got dressed that day.

A Part of You Knows Better, But . . .

The problem isn't that you dated the Workout Guy or even that you spent a few months feeling superior to the rest of the human race; the problem is that you may feel bad about it afterward. You fancy yourself a nice person and you don't seek out people to whom you can feel superior. You simply need to recognize that you were at a time in your life when your ego was bruised, and you took the shortest route to gain some momentum. Just know that once you do start feeling better about yourself, you will wake up and realize that endless discussion of bodybuilding as an athletic endeavor versus bodybuilding as a sport is really not your bag. Marc Jacobs's is.

Meet Chelsea, a perpetual Workout Guy dater. Chelsea is from a very wealthy family: her great-grandfather was in shipping, so money, and all the focus on glamour and appearances that comes along with it, has been a part of her life for a couple of generations now. Despite her history of privilege, Chelsea's parents taught her the value of hard work, and made sure that she always had a summer job while she was in school. Now in her late twenties and a product of her generation, Chelsea has tried on several different career hats. With each one, she managed to find herself a different Workout Guy boyfriend: when she was a makeup artist, she dated a baseball player she met at a photo shoot; when she was a photographer for a travel magazine, she met a whitewater-rafting instructor in Fiji. Most recently, Chelsea has landed in the music industry, where she worked for a few years before asking her father to help her start her own music management company. Chelsea's music-industry-appropriate dating choice? A $300-an-hour personal trainer. And by "dating" we mean "sleeping together," as well as dragging this particular Workout Guy to society events.

As Chelsea approached thirty, she took stock of her dating life, and began to recognize the inherent shallowness of so many of the industries was involved in. She was distressed to realize that she fell for all of that shallowness, hook, line, and sinker, by only dating athletic hunks who never really impacted her life. How could she have wasted her twenties doing nothing in particular and creating nothing substantive? She had little to show for her dating escapades: no real bonds and no relationship worth having. Years of dating these guys had left her feeling empty, and she became very depressed.

Like many women who indulge in the Workout Guy mentality, Chelsea became too comfortable in a superficial mode of thinking about life. Yes, in moderation it is liberating to completely immerse yourself in your superficial side. At some point, though, you must realize that life is bigger than looks. If dating a guy who is as two-dimensional as they come adds *some* dimension to your life, then that is a good thing. You got a chance to see how the other half lived, and let's face it, it sucked. Now you can really appreciate all aspects of people, and you understand that looking your very best is an empty experience if you are not fulfilled inside.

The Workout Guy comfort level can be enticing. He, like some of the other *Been There, Done That* guys, allows you to not have to think too much. That's fine, until you realize you want more from your life and from your relationships.

 *your jewel of wisdom*

Well, maybe this wasn't the crown jewel in your jewelry box, and maybe he didn't have much in the family jewels department either. He was more of a strong alloy than a shiny emerald. Still, there are lessons to be learned all around. Studies show that women don't put as much importance on men's physical appearance as one would think, but if that's true, then why did you date a guy who is all about his own physical appearance? Why date someone more obsessed with his body than with yours? Was it just his overall grooming that you liked? What were some of his worst qualities, which you were happy to be rid of? This dumbbell could be worth his weight in gold if dating him lets you add another gem to your Essentials List.

chapter nine
the party guy

personality profile

You will know when you've met the Party Guy, or, as he refers to himself, "the party animal," which is appropriate because he runs in herds. He is never alone, as he needs a constant stream of spectators for his wacky shenanigans. He is a social being and that's about it. You won't have many private moments with the Party Guy (even in the shower; he has a webcam). If it doesn't concern others, it doesn't concern him. The objective to being the Party Guy is to entertain the troops, which can be anyone from the waitresses at dinner to his coworkers at a meeting. He likes tall drinks, tall tales, and tall people (because he thinks it's funny to trip them) and he *lives* for April Fools' Day.

He always sees the keg as half full

When you were a freshman in college and your life looked like an MTV Spring Break episode, this guy was tons of fun, because he always saw the keg as half full. The Party Guy's condition may also be referred to as "the Peter Pan Syndrome." He is the ever-popular eternal frat boy who still needs his mandatory number of nights out each week with his friends—at age thirty-two! His idea of fun is the "recreational use" of certain drugs, and he *doesn't* think that constitutes a problem. The Party Guy drinks a little too much, tells war stories about college conquests, and owns a beer bong. White Party Guy is the worst; he's a cross between a gangsta rapper and an M.B.A. The most gangsta thing about him is that his mother bought him an Eminem CD for Christmas. Word to her. The Party Guy has hooked up with most of your friends at least once, and if you leave him alone for too long at a party he will disappear into the abyss, but still somehow manage to end up on your doorstep at 4 a.m., puking in your hydrangea. When you met him you had the vague feeling that you may have slept with him before, about a year ago (thus making him a deja screw.) You started dating him this time around because you got tired of running into him at parties and taking him home just to watch him get sick in your bathroom. Hey, the Party Guy is actually kind of cute, and you think to yourself that another round with him could be fun! And that's what the Party Guy is all about: fun. He's not so good at one-on-one, but you try anyhow. You even attempt to take him out for a grown-up dinner with your friends, and though you remind him to use his inside voice with relentless patience, he ends up loud, drunk, and French-kissing the waitress (and if he's had tequila, the waiter). Come on, you have to know that *that* relationship has an expiration date.

Karen's Party Guy, Brian, couldn't have been more her opposite. She is petite, pretty, and conservative; he is an ex–football player, well over six feet tall, close to 250 pounds, and rough around the edges. But whenever they hung out, Karen and Brian had a blast together. Karen may be small, but the girl can drink, and she had no trouble keeping up with her Party Guy's carousing ways. Their favorite activity was to head to the seaport every Friday evening to eat oysters and clams, and imbibe several

a history of dating

today

People are getting married later and later as the decades roll on. To borrow a slogan from the old cigarette ads, "You've come a long way, baby." The main point is that you can take the pressure off and be happy knowing that you are, right now, part of a brand-new attitude and a brand-new era when it comes to dating and men. No one can really define what that attitude is for you; it is whatever you want it to be. Maybe it is cohabiting and never marrying; maybe it's dating lots of men and waiting to marry until you are absolutely sure of who you are and what you want. I don't know what the idea of romance and partnering is for you, but what I do know is that we will look back and say that this time was a time like no other.

pitchers of beer before going home for hours of great sex. Karen and Brian weren't *close* necessarily, but they laughed a lot and shared some parts of their lives with each other over those pitchers and clams. Mostly they regaled each other with stories about getting drunk with other people. After a while, Karen's Friday nights with Brian became something of an institution, and as

ring-ring!

You know you are dating the Party Guy when the phone call for a Saturday night date goes like this:

SCENARIO It's Tuesday night, the phone rings and all you hear is "You gotta fight . . . for your right . . . to paaarrrttttyy" but under the loud music you think you hear Party Guy yelling "HELLO? HELLO?"

you: Hey, I can barely hear you. Speak up!

him: OH . . . (yelling) YOU WANNA GOWOUTSATRDYNT

you: What?

him: (yelling) DO YOU WANT TO GO OUT SATURDAY NIGHT?

you: Sure

him: (yelling) WHAT??

you: SURE

him: (yelling) WHAT??!!!

you: WHY DON'T YOU CALL ME WHEN YOU GET HOME.

him: I AM HOME.

Let's not kid ourselves with how this SHOULD have gone. If you were honest, you wouldn't be dating him in the first place.

soon as the end of the week would roll around, she'd find herself looking forward to kicking off the weekend with him.

If you're like Karen and most other Party Guy daters, spending time with the Party Guy reminds you of an easier time in life, when you didn't have any responsibilities. "Who cares that he's thirty-five?" you think. He's livin' *la vida loca*, and being with him is a great escape from the drudgery of daily life! Unfortunately you are too busy having fun to even think critically about your relationship, and most of the time you are out on the town, partying with other people. Even if you do talk the Party Guy into staying in, it only means that you two play drinking games like beer-shots-backgammon or Jack Daniels poker (it doesn't matter what you call it, all of the games are about taking a shot when you lose a round).

Party Guy-isms

When you're with the Party Guy, you never think about where your relationship is heading or if he's your Mr. Right; you are just trying to stay sober long enough to call your mother back. The Party Guy can sense that you're an intelligent lady, and when he's with you, he pretends to have a sensitive side, because he thinks it's what you want him to do. He doesn't really *know* he's pretending; he's just trying to relate to you one-on-one in a meaningful way, and it's ineffectual because relating to women is something that the Party Guy has never really mastered. You see, you aren't like the other girls he knows, who spend their time doing their hair and their nails, gossiping, screwing, dieting, and tanning. His sisters are like that too, except for his one sister who wants to be a photographer and is considered the "weirdo" of the family. In the back of his mind, he can't shake the feeling that his attempts at being sensitive with you may have something to do with being arty, too, and that is just weird.

The Party Guy likes to show up unannounced; he is a whirlwind of fun and frolic like that. One day he's at your door in a T-shirt that reads, "24 hours in a day, 24 beers in a case, coincidence?" and whisks you off to the beach for the weekend to go out on some guy's boat with seventeen other random people, none of whom are couples. As it happens, he barely knows the guy who owns the boat: he was out one night and the guy next to him said, "You're an animal! You should come out on my boat some time," and there you are. Still, you have a blast cruising around open waters with a bunch of strangers, and you even meet this one cool girl that you totally connect with and decide to e-mail once you are back on dry land. The Party Guy is good for that. In fact, you met several of your close friends through him, and whenever you guys reminisce about that now, it's always a funny story, because none of you has spoken to the Party Guy in years.

You may jokingly call the Party Guy a "frat boy" but make no mistake, he really was in a fraternity at school. That's where he learned his most comprehensive lessons in degrading and objectifying women; it's practically written in the bylaws. The Party Guy was actually attending school when they first instituted those drinking rules for the Greek system, so he didn't really get his fill. The grand irony is that the Party Guy is actually *terrible* at drinking: he has a low tolerance, can't hold his liquor, and inevitably ends up a drunken mess whenever he goes out. But he's the Party Guy—why let that stop him? The Party Guy

ten items you hope to never see, but that are in the
···party guy's apartment anyway ····

1. The al dente spaghetti testing wall
2. A pizza box from five weeks ago with mail inside of it from three weeks ago
3. Beer cans from all over the world
4. Notches on his bedpost—oh sorry, that's *nachos*
5. A real live condom dispenser in his bedroom
6. A bong shaped as a keg, and vice versa
7. The "bra wall"
8. The Party Guy haggling with a tranny over $20
9. His floor
10. A nice family of rodents

is different from your other boyfriends because after you break up with him, you will continue to say "hi" and maybe even flirt with him once again. On the other hand, you may also throw a drink in his face, depending on the version of the story about you that he told to his friends. Party Guy is notorious for not being able to rise to the occasion after he's got a few drinks in him, but he would never admit this. (It's not that you are a size queen, but the first time you saw what whiskey had done to his manhood you exclaimed, "You couldn't even hurt my feelings with that thing!") There's no middle ground with the Party Guy. Just remember these things: He is more familiar with the term "license and registration" than he is with the term "girlfriend," he actually knows what a barroom floor tastes like, and several times he has woken up naked in strange places, not knowing

···in a nutshell ····························

the fantasy Party Guy may be a little over the top, but he is still a great, unselfish, passionate lover.

the harsh reality His days of wine and roses will soon become months of dialysis and Viagra.

how you broke up He came over one night and saw that you were out of beer. You never saw him again.

where he is or where his clothes are. Is this the guy who will be the father of your children? Let's hope not.

Why You Dated the Party Guy in the First Place

You were immature yourself. Let's face it, you were like a little mad scientist experimenting with the depths of your party abilities, the limits of your alcohol consumption, and the level to which you would sink just to say that you had a boyfriend. After all, drunk sex is better than no sex, right? The Party Guy was an important part of your development as a woman of the world. He was the guy you got drunk with and then capsized the catamaran on the Chesapeake Bay, he was the guy you got drunk and camped out in line with for Rolling Stones tickets, and he was the guy who got drunk with and well . . . didn't do anything special really; he's just your drinking buddy. He is, however, the guy who taught you that beer and liquor do indeed mix if you stretch out the night long enough. This is very valuable information.

You've always known that that one day you would be a wife, an executive, and even a mommy . . . but just not yet. The Party Guy was your chance to be wild and rebel against all of that pesky structure you grew up with. Back in the day your mother did the same thing (though she won't admit it.) She dated the dangerous guy who wore leather and drove some Satan-mobile or perhaps smoked. In this day and age guys like that seem to have become big pansies, and we refer to them now as "frat boys" instead of "bad boys," but the rebellious sentiment is still there. They may have traded Harleys for Hardees but they are still squeezing the ketchup all over the table and running out without paying the check. This breed of boy is still bad—just not really *dangerous*. After all, their parents spent a lot of money on braces, and it would be a shame to chip a tooth if they can avoid it.

A Part of You Knows Better, But . . .

You wanted to be bad too! You wanted to test your limits, but after a while, it got old. That's why when you broke up with the Party Guy it didn't seem like it was that big of a deal. What you didn't realize was that on a more profound level, it most certainly was. Dating the Party Guy in the first place spoke volumes about your self-esteem: Why did you allow this guy into your life for so long? Yes, you may have walked the party animal walk yourself, but you also let someone think of you as a playmate and not a girl to be reckoned with. And you deserved so much more than that. It's true, you had fun with the Party Guy, but a little part of you inside was hurt on a deeper level, and it took you some time to recover.

Don't believe me? Then look at the next few guys you dated after the Party Guy. Your next relationships were no healthier, because while you may not have been looking for a husband at that point in your life, you also weren't looking for respect. Your hangover from the Party Guy took its toll despite the amounts of aspirin, cold pizza, and Yoo-hoo you consumed.

When Marnie was thirty-four, she thought she was simply dating a fun, popular guy who liked his Jägermeister a little too much. She found out the hard way that she was accidentally dating the Party Guy. They got drunk together on their first couple of dates but, at first, she just chalked that up to nerves. On their second date, he asked if she was a runner, and when she replied that she was, he invited her to a Hash Race, telling her that he was a harrier. Marnie had even done a mini-marathon here and there, so she thought this could be fun—even though she didn't really know who the "Hash Race Harriers" were. To Marnie's surprise, the Hash Race Harriers turned out to be an offbeat social club that mixed running to no place in particular with beer drinking. The only goal these runners had, athletic or otherwise, was to get really, really drunk. The Party Guy did this almost every weekend. He was an alcoholic with a really good pair of New Balance shoes. Furthermore, what Marnie first thought was a fun and exciting guy with a big personality who liked to be center of attention turned out to be a somewhat pathetic guy who used booze to mask his inability to be real. Every time she tried to have a real conversation with him, he either made her feel stupid for asking anything personal, or he just changed the subject. Try as she could, she never connected with him, and for good reason—she'd mistakenly gotten tangled up with the Party Guy.

signs that your date with
· party guy is not going well ·········

- ◆ When you comment on his vivacious personality he replies, "Oh . . . I do whip-its before I go out."
- ◆ The bumper sticker on his car reads: "Life, Liberty, and the Pursuit of Happy Hour!"
- ◆ It takes you over an hour to find a bar to go to that he wasn't banned from.
- ◆ Right before you get into his car he exclaims, "Hang on, let me just make sure my will is in order first."

Don't mistake the Party Guy for someone who just loves life and is trying to take it lightly. Much of the time his carefree attitude is masking some real pain, and you do not want to be around when those floodgates open, if they ever do. You cannot have a real relationship with the Party Guy. He may not actually be an alcoholic, but for now all of those kegs are cheaper than the therapy he will desperately need if he ever decides to grow up. When he finally stops self-medicating—or in this case, self-lubricating—he will realize that he is 5' 6", totally average looking, and that his paycheck is not just extra beer money. If in fact the Party Guy is an alcoholic or an addict of some kind, you have a long road ahead of you. It would be one thing if you had a significant relationship with a person who had an addiction problem. The Party Guy, however, isn't that person; instead he is someone you don't really connect with, and who would not be there for you if you ever needed him. The Party Guy will make this clear to you in small

First of all, a good shrink would tell him to leave her office and tell his problems to his bartender. However, if she wanted to really get to the bottom of things she would say that there may be a number of reasons why he is the Party Guy.

While we know that ultimately you were never going to be with him, you did date him for a while because, let's admit it, it's intoxicating (pun intended) to be with the life of the party. When you're on the arm of the guy everyone likes, to whom everybody pays attention, you are liked, by proxy. But what the Party Guy may be masking could amount to something a lot more serious, especially if he is a substance abuser or has Histrionic Personality Disorder. Since hardly anyone has a substance abuse problem in a vacuum, he is most likely suffering from both of these problems rolled up into one, meaning that there is a reason for his substance dependency. He is self-medicating with alcohol instead of getting to the bottom of what he is running away from, which explains his intimacy issues too. If he has a majority of these symptoms, he is also histrionic:

◆ *He is uncomfortable if he is not the center of attention:* He doesn't just like to be the life of the party; he *has* to be life of the party. All of those funny hats and all of those loud shirts and big gestures are not just bad fashion choices—they are designed to call attention to himself.

◆ *His interaction with women is generally sexual or, at least, provocative:* He doesn't relate to women in any *real* way;

it's always got to have something to do with their tits or their butts. Don't think so? He likes to snap the bras and G-strings of strange women, so what does that tell ya?

◆ *He's a bit shallow:* "A bit" is an understatement; he makes Paris Hilton look like Hillary Clinton.

◆ *He uses his physical being to draw attention to himself:* All of that awkward dancing in inappropriate places is not just his being an all-around fun Party Guy. It's a cry for help!

◆ *He is the drunken drama king:* He needs to be the center of attention in every setting and if he is not, he will create a reason to be. When you were celebrating passing the bar, he made loud jokes all night that started with "Me? I could never pass a bar, I have to go right in!" or "It's good to know a lawyer, but it's hard to break the law if you're completely passed out!"

◆ *He is easily influenced:* Sure, there are some nights when he says he is just not going to party, that he needs a night off, but his friends know they can always talk him into shots of tequila or a keg or two.

◆ *He considers superficial relationships to be closer than they actually are:* While the bartender at Smitty McGee's may actually know the Party Guy, they are not best friends. Nor is the Party Guy great friends with Rob Lowe because he had a beer with him while he was filming *St. Elmo's Fire* at his college back in the '80s.

but significant ways. Think about the day when you asked him to be your date for a friend's party, and he made up some lame excuse for why he couldn't make it, when you knew the only reason he wouldn't come was because none of his friends were going to be there. The Party Guy's logic: Why should he waste a night with you and your friends when his boys may be doing something cool, or better yet, sitting around doing nothing at all?

Karen learned this about her Party Guy's agenda the hard way. While she told herself at first that Brian was just another one of the guys she was dating, she in truth hoped for more with him. Karen considered him special in a way, and thought in the back of her mind that when she was done dating around, she might take Brian a little more seriously. Then one day Karen and her roommate had a huge blowout fight. They had been fighting for weeks, but this was a major argument that sent her storming out of the house in anger. The first person Karen thought to dial for some support was Brian. She called him, crying, looking for a little sympathy and a place to crash for the night. Brian's reaction was quite the contrary—he acted as though he had no idea who she was or why she was calling him. He made some lame excuse about why she couldn't come over, and then rushed her off the phone, saying he was late for a kegger. Karen was shocked. How could this sweet teddy bear of the Friday night rendezvous be so cold, and exhibit so little compassion for her? In that moment Karen realized that Brian was all about the fun and the sex and the party, and he was not the least bit interested in her real problems. Sure, she could complain about her father or a coworker to him over a pitcher of beer, but little did she know that Brian was only half listening, and 100 percent not caring. No sooner did she need him (in the most innocuous of ways, mind you) than his true colors came out. It wasn't as if she was asking him for a real favor, like to help her move or paint her house; she was just looking for a place to sleep and a shoulder to cry on. The Party Guy couldn't offer even that.

It's a typical Party Guy move to only be there for the good times. Imagine if you had a death in the family or some really serious problems. If you did, this would not be the go-to guy. This is the main reason you can only date the Party Guy for a short period of time. You may start to get attached, and maybe even dream of making the Party Guy into something more than he really is, but you must understand that he isn't now and never will be, able to be that for you. He is flawed and incapable of anything more than teaching you how to chug a boilermaker, or knowing where all the good festivities are tonight. Sure, the Party Guy has his reasons for making his priorities himself and his own hedonistic pleasures, but the bottom line is, it doesn't really matter what those reasons are. His disinterest in all things substantive should scream out to you that he isn't interested in a serious relationship, and this may be true for a long time to come. The main question you should be asking yourself is this: How can you possibly think that a guy like this is husband material, and not the poster child for the Betty Ford Clinic?

◈ *your jewel of wisdom*

The case of the Party Guy is a clear case of pearls before swine. So, your pearl of wisdom here relates to the timing of this relationship. That should really tell you a lot about where you were in your life when you dated him. You may not need to add this lesson to your Essentials List, because maturity could have taken care of it for you, but just in case this is still your MO, let's examine. Are you dating men with the Party Guy lifestyle because you don't think you deserve better than someone who has no respect for himself? How intense is his partying? Look at all aspects of this and the "why" behind the swine, and you will have something of worth to add to your list.

PART FOUR

the jewelry box

You've *Been There, Done That*, and look at the jewels of wisdom you have to show for it! We've reviewed the ghosts of your relationships past; now it's time to put that knowledge to work for you, and to figure out how it's going to shape your relationship future. But if you don't take the time to focus on yourself, you run the risk of falling into the same patterns of your dating past. This is your opportunity to think about who *you* are and what *you* want, remembering that the choices that you make now shape the rest of your life. In this section we'll comb through your jewelry box, determine which pieces will enhance your life, and which need to go. We'll also add some valuable pieces, like jewels that you'd buy yourself, without which no woman's collection would be complete. The next section is devoted to you, because no matter who is in your life, remember that the most precious jewel in your possession is you—you are your own most valuable asset. ❧

chapter ten

your essentials list: a primer

By now you're probably asking yourself, "What the heck is the Essentials List anyway?" The Essentials List is like an inventory of the things that are *so* important to you that your relationship will not work without them. These are the personality traits or behaviors that the man for you needs to exhibit in order to call him The One; the qualities that will make you the happiest you can be, and will ultimately sustain your relationship. In other words, your Essentials List is your list of ultimate dealbreakers.

As you may have noticed, I keep referring to "you" and "your relationship," and this is for good reason. The most important aspect of the Essentials List, as you will see, is that it is as individual and unique as you are. Nobody else has the exact same past that you do, and nobody has the exact same needs that you have. There may be women out there with similar criteria for Mr. Right, or shared misadventures in the dating trenches, but these experiences will not affect you in the exact same way. The key to the Essentials List, the reason it is such an effective tool, is that

·· why make a list? ··························

Science, really. Research has shown that when people develop a clear plan of action to reach a goal they tend to get there faster than someone who has not put a distinctive plan together. Making a list is one of the fastest and most linear ways to achieve your goals. Goal-setting works best when you set up smaller goals in service of the big one, which in this case is finding love. But also there is experience (yours) that should lead you to the understanding that the items on your list must be so important to you, that without them your relationship cannot survive!

the items on your list are not random suggestions or philosophies about dating cobbled together from the advice of your friends or from a magazine. In order to identify the items on your Essentials List, you need to look closely at your dating history and figure out what went wrong in your past relationships. You need to determine what you really want from your future relationships, and what you will not settle for. With the Essentials List in hand you can tell immediately if your latest guy will stack up. The number of items on your Essentials List is ultimately up to you. After talking to hundreds of women, my research has shown that the ideal length for the list is no fewer than four items and no more than seven. Here are some other research statistics that I thought you might find interesting:

◆ 88 percent of the women I spoke with rated personality as being more important to them than looks.

- 35 percent said that they will only date Younger Guys, but the U.S. Census says that only 12 percent of marriages in the United States are between older women and younger men (so 23 percent of you had better rethink that list!)
- 20 percent of the women said they do not have an alcoholic drink on the first date because they want to "be completely lucid," "not give him an excuse to take advantage sexually," and they "think it sends a bad message."
- 76 percent of the women I interviewed said that their goal in making their Essentials List was to try to not be fooled by the external stuff they see when they first meet a guy (his resume, so to speak).

   The remaining 24 percent said that their goal in finally getting serious about finding The One ranged from fear of being alone to being ready to settle down and have children.
- 91 percent of the women I interviewed who were dating at the time of the interview but had recently broken up with someone said that at least one thing on their list made them break up with their boyfriends. 18 percent said that more than two items on their list were the reason that things went wrong.

So, you see? The Essentials List really works! What you will find is that, if you get your list right, it will become your dating bible. You will be able to predict how the relationship will go and in what areas it is lagging, and it will hold true each time you enter into a new relationship. If a man meets all but one of the criteria on your Essentials List, it will be because of that one outstanding reason that you eventually (and inevitably) break up. These are dealbreakers in the truest sense of the word: I am talking about stuff that you cannot live with, or live without. Hang in there; you'll see what I mean.

Developing a Master Plan

To get started, let's first define what it is you'll be doing in this section. It has been my experience, both as a psychologist and as a woman who dated for many years, many, many—okay, you get the point—that until you know exactly what you are looking for, you have no way of knowing:

- That you have found it.
- Where to even begin to look.

Now, here's the hard part: You have to figure out what your Essentials are on your own. There is no set list that I can give you; it is entirely up to you to create your list, based on your own personal history, past experiences, and your specific personality. That is where *Been There, Done That, Kept the Jewelry* comes in. By carefully examining why your previous relationships did not work, you can figure out exactly what you want / need / can't live without in the future. What was it like to look at some of the *Been There, Done That* guys? Was there a glimmer of recognition? Possibly a blinding glare of recognition? The cause of your breakup, and the types of guys you chose to date, are hints for items that need to be on your list. If you recognized a lot of yourself in many of the women in parts 1 through 3, that's totally cool—mistakes are how we learn, right? The point, though, is that you are no longer interested in wasting your time with guys who aren't right for you. You have sat around long enough waiting for phone calls, waiting for plans to be made, and waiting for the right guy to come along. You have had your last Clingy Guy, your last Workout Guy, and this is the last straw.

mr. oh-so-wrong

It's easy to choose the wrong guys. We have all done it, and we know when we are doing it. Hindsight is always 20/20, but here are few extreme examples of the Top 5 Mr. Wrong stories I encountered in the course of my research:

- "When I went to see him in his band, he had more makeup on than I did."
- "I didn't mind taking off my shoes the first time I went to his apartment, but two things freaked me out. One was when he reminded me to refold the towel and then place it in the hamper. And two, when he made me use hand sanitizer before touching him."
- "On our first date, before we went to dinner, I ran up to his place to use the bathroom. When I came out he was naked and holding a twenty-dollar bill and asked me which I'd rather have. I took the money."
- "After two dates with this one guy, he called me about a week later and it sounded really echo-y, so I asked where he was calling from and he said, 'jail.'"
- "He kept his appliances in the refrigerator."

You have reached a turning point, sister.

Turning Points

We all reach our turning points at different times. I reached mine when I turned thirty. At the time, I was in a relationship with a classic Younger Guy. He was sexy as hell, smart and funny, and I kept thinking, "In five (or more like twenty) years he will be SUCH a catch; but right now he is just too silly!" At first it was fun to wake up on Saturday mornings with him, eat pancakes, and watch cartoons. However, when I realized that what I thought was a kitschy, alternative way to spend my weekend mornings was his real life, I began to panic. I was looking for a man, and here I was with a boy! Oh sure, I could screw around with silly men who were wrong for me at twenty-nine, but no thirty-year-old worth her salt would waste another minute. That's when I knew it was over.

Turning thirty was my shining moment. I have to admit that at that time, I myself had certainly *Been There, Done That*. I probably dated all of the guys described here, not to mention my escapades with Long Distance Guy, Mama's Boy, and Most Likely to Be Gay Guy, but that's another book. Anyway, it was when I decided to start getting a little more serious about the men with whom I became intimate that things really began to change. While I knew that I didn't want to take the fun out of it, I also knew that I would soon be thirty-five, and that if I wanted to get married or have kids, I'd better get on the ball (no pun intended.)

I felt bold when I broke up with the Younger Guy. I didn't have a relationship safety net; there was no Hot Guy, or any guy

·· feminist disclaimer ················

Just to be clear, I am referring to women who do not want to go through life alone in this instance. I'm a feminist, third wave, thank you, and I am all for women not being in relationships or being in ones that are not going to end in marriage or long-term commitment. I am not talking about those women. I'm talking about women who really want to be a twosome, but have had a hell of a time in their quest; the ones who are ready to try something different.

for that matter, waiting in the wings. I was brave and very independent. It had occurred to me that I might very well be alone for a long time, maybe even the rest of my life. But for the first time that thought was freeing, not frightening. Ah, thirty. It was then that it occurred to me that my relationship future was actually in *my* hands. It was not up to men to decide whether they wanted me or not. I could decide what I wanted and didn't want, and when I met someone who didn't have qualities that I respected or felt were imperative in a relationship, I would move on. No grass growing under my feet. I followed my own advice: I sat down to write out what I absolutely wanted from my Mr. Right (and what I most certainly did not want), and I didn't stop until I found him. And just so I don't leave you hanging, I did find him, and I married him. Forever is what I was looking for; you might be looking for something else. You may just want a healthy relationship. The idea is that, either way, *you* decide rather than letting chance, or (heaven forbid) a guy who could be Mr. Wrong, decide for you.

Remember in the beginning when we talked about individuality? That is the "Essential" part, really. You as an individual have had experiences that have led you to this moment right now. No two women have had the exact same experiences, even if you dated the exact same guy. Let's look at best friends Cynthia and Nadine, both of whom dated the same Bachelor. Of course, the Bachelor is true to his name, and neither Cynthia nor Nadine is still with him. What is interesting is that the relationship itself went very differently for both women. Cynthia's personality elicited certain responses from him that Nadine's did not. Cynthia was shy with the Bachelor, while Nadine, a total party girl whose favorite thing to do is hang at Bungalow 8, tends to be more aggressive and fun-loving. So with Cynthia, the Bachelor took charge of their plans more and was also more sexual, since she made him feel at ease.

With Nadine the Bachelor was uncharacteristically open about his life, because she forced him to talk more than Cynthia had. And while Nadine and the Bachelor had a really great time together, he was less sexual because she was a bit overbearing. Not that any of it matters—the Bachelor was never going to get serious with either one of them anyway—but the point here is that Nadine and Cynthia both had unique reasons for dating the Bachelor in the first place, and equally diverse experiences while they were with him. This is what I am getting at: you, as an individual, have very specific needs that others do not.

By this point in your dating life, you probably have a good, though rough, idea of what you may or may not settle for in a relationship. But writing the Essentials List is going to force you to get a lot more specific than that. The key is that you need to figure out those things that you will not, *under any circumstances*, settle for. This is serious stuff we're talking about here—not just the "should have sense of humor and blue eyes" kind of stuff, but also the real stuff that's hiding beneath the surface. Your list needs to contain identities and personality traits that have real consequence for you. For example, "I need a guy who is not judgmental of any part of my life" will serve you better than, "I need a guy who looks good on my arm."

Getting Started

The main point that is crucial to understand is that women who are single and don't want to be are most likely single because they are choosing the wrong guys. It may seem so obvious: "Yes, duh, thank you; I'm single because I have been with the wrong guys, no kidding." But now it's time to accept, move on, and figure out the "why" behind your bad-guy choices. Why have you been dating the wrong guys? Are you aware of it but doing it anyway? Do you think that the right guy isn't out there, so you date to not be lonely? Maybe you think great guys are out there but that they would never be interested in you. If you can get to the root of this, you can get a handle on what it is you are really looking for, and who it is that will contribute to your life in the very best way.

It's the leap to asking yourself why you dated the wrong guys that I want you to make. There are several ways to go about figuring this out. Start by asking yourself these questions:

- What broke up your last relationship? What broke up the one before that?

- What are some relationship patterns that you have been dying to break?
- What guys have you chosen that you *knew* have been wrong but you dated anyway?
- Why did you continue to date Mr. Wrong? What were you really looking for?

If you can answer these questions honestly, then you're well on your way to figuring out what your Essentials are. You'll see that maybe it wasn't his inability to tell a joke, unless of course you want to marry a standup comic. We will answer these questions (and more!) in the next chapter.

From Breakup to Dealbreaker

So, you've been ruminating on *why* your last few relationships broke up. Now it's time to extrapolate your dealbreakers from that knowledge. Consider the "research" you've done about your last few breakups. For example, Rachel's last relationship broke up because her boyfriend, Alan, wasn't very good at expressing how he really felt about her, or about life, or about anything, really. He wasn't a good communicator and it drove her crazy. Like Rachel, perhaps you are the kind of gal who likes a good heart-to-heart every now and then. So, now you know that your list like Rachel's should include "A guy who is great at communicating." What goes with that is "A guy who is not afraid to be vulnerable." If you are the kind of woman who isn't really into a guy expressing his feelings, then those suggestions would not apply to you. They would not be on your Essentials List. There are no rules here, other than getting to the heart of what you really need. You cannot go by what works for someone else or by the clichéd idea of what a woman *should* want; you have to put on your list exactly what you *do* want. You may like a nonexpressive chap, and you may think that too much emotion is corny coming from a guy. You may not be comfortable with expressing every little thing that you feel at every given moment. That is totally cool, and the exact idea that I am trying to get across. The Essentials List is as discrete and as completely unique as you are.

One Woman's DUH Is Another Woman's Essential

Don't censor yourself! While something like "don't date a heroin addict" may be a big "DUH" for you, it's been an issue with Briana. She has had her share of hurt puppies (Wounded Guys), and no matter how hard she tries, she can never fix them. Yet she continues to date them, and then wonders why the relationships don't work out. She needs to have at the top of her list, "No more guys who need fixing; time to date one who isn't broken." What may be a "DUH" moment for you may be something big and important on someone else's list. Heck, it could even be number one!

Don't feel bashful about what you want. This list is for you and you only. You can hide your list, you can hide this book—I don't care, I just want you to be happy. Sometimes it is in your private moments and with your own private thoughts that you find the most clarity. So keep this personal, share it, don't share it, it's your choice. Just don't censor yourself. If you need yellow roses on Tuesdays, then write it in big letters on your list: "I WANT A GUY WHO WILL BRING ME YELLOW ROSES ON TUESDAYS." And while perhaps when out at a party you don't want to advertise that you only date Barry Manilow fans (or as we lovingly call them, Fanilows) but if a shared affinity for Barry Manilow is something that you really, truly want in your guy, by all means, put it on your list! It is nobody's business but your own what will make you happy, no matter how unusual your request may seem. It's yours, and that's the idea.

Mr. Right Is in the Details

The more specific and detailed you are about your list, the better. Kirsten, for example, is a big Wounded Guy dater. No matter how stoic her men may seem when she first meets them, they almost always end up having mommy issues or manic-depressive tendencies that surface, usually around month three of the relationship. The Wounded Guys are drawn to her nurturing nature like moths to flame. Now, Kirsten truly likes being with sensitive guys, so she should definitely put "I need a guy who is really in touch with his feelings" on her list. But she should also include more specific parameters, perhaps writing something like "I need a guy who is in touch with his feelings but not to the extent that he is needy." If Kirsten just writes, "I need a guy who is really in touch with his feelings," she runs the risk of dating Wounded Guys again and again, who, because of some cosmic riddle that they are trying to answer, are in touch with only their negative feelings at the exclusion of everything else. She may also land a guy who is in touch with only one feeling: grief, sadness, or despair. No, Kirsten doesn't want anything to do with any of that. Nor do you. You are looking for a guy who can say what he is really feeling because he is trying to connect with you and further your relationship, not because he is desperate or damaged in any way. This guarantees a more mutual exchange rather than you playing shrink and ending up in another imbalanced liaison.

Getting It Done

Next are stories about a few women who have created their Essentials List. First I want to thank them for allowing me to include their specific lists in this book as examples to help you. Interestingly, when I met these lovely ladies, each one of them chalked up the failure of her past relationships to stuff that was entirely out of her control. ("I was having a string of bad luck" or "The right guy was never around.") After they sat down and made their lists they realized that, not only did they have patterns that needed to be changed, but also that they could control what they would and would not accept. One had told me that she settled because she was embarrassed to ask for what she really wanted; another said that she had never thought about her needs in this way but that after she made her list, it made perfect sense to her. See what you think.

Caroline's Story

Meet Caroline, my kind of girl—a Younger Guy dater. That's her thing, and she says that she just can't do anything about it. She's attracted to Younger Guys and that is that. Caroline is

·· before you date 'em? ··········

1. A guy who you've seen but don't know starts hanging around you a little more and has been paying lots of attention to you. Your friends say that he's dated half the town and is a bit of a player, but he's not like that with you. When he asks you out, you:
   a. Go if you have nothing else to do; otherwise, why bother?
   b. Trust your girls and don't go out with him; you'll meet someone else.
   c. Go out with him. It's how he treats *you* that matters.

2. At the movies you see Sam, a guy you've had two dates with, but now he is with another girl. You figure:
   a. He's obviously not interested.
   b. You only had two dates; he can do what he wants and so can you . . . as a matter of fact . . . you have a dinner thing later on.
   c. March over to where he is sitting and ask Sam to explain himself.

3. A guy who you have been flirting with lately walks right by as you are standing a foot away from the ticket window where they are selling limited engagement U2 tickets. You:
   a. Smile, say hi, and then go back to talking with your friend.
   b. Yell out, "Hey what took you so long, get over here!"
   c. Wave and sarcastically say, "Have fun in the nosebleed section!"

4. Your boss has asked you to pick a partner for a project. There is a sexy, hunky, very eligible guy in your office. You:
   a. Pick someone other than hunky guy; after all, you don't stand a chance with him, so why tease yourself?
   b. Approach said hunk in a businesslike way and when he agrees to work with you, mildly turn on the charm.
   c. Pick the person who is a friend of hunky eligible guy and impress the hell out of him. He'll do your bidding for you with hunky guy.

5. Your third date with him is after a ten-hour day during which you had to stand for most of the time. Your date says:

  a. "Why don't you find a job where you're not on your feet as much?"

  b. "Lucky you, I give the best foot massage in town."

  c. "I hope you changed your shoes, your feet probably smell, ha ha!"

6. It's the dreaded third date and he is looking for some between-the-sheets action. When you make it clear that you are not ready, your perfect guy would:

  a. Give you those gorgeous puppy-dog eyes till you decide, rules, shmoolz, you have needs too!

  b. Be a bit disappointed, but he will wait till you are ready.

  c. Start pouting and calling you frigid.

7. Come clean . . . the thing that you like most about him is:

  a. He is the babe of the century and every girl you know wants him, but *you* got him!

  b. He makes you feel beautiful and smart.

  c. He holds a mirror up to your face (figuratively) and makes you really take a look at who you are.

8. On your second date you manage to spill wine on your blouse, light the menu on fire, and say "shit!" so loud that a child at the next table heard it. The guy you will go on a third date with would:

  a. Laugh hysterically.

  b. Lean forward and jokingly say, "You didn't tell me I would need an insurance policy to go out with you."

  c. Who cares, you're too busy flirting with the cute waiter, who finds your antics adorable.

continued

9. You think you're coming down with—cough, cough—the flu. Even though you just started dating, he should:

   a. Stay away; he has a big week next week and can't get sick right now.

   b. Come over with some vitamin C and some flowers.

   c. Who cares what he'll do; you're trying to get better

10. His best friend:

    a. Won a belching contest at your local pub.

    b. Is his business partner in a new venture that seems to be going really well.

    c. Is kinda cute . . . and if your guy wasn't so sensitive, you'd date the friend too.

Mostly a's: Hit or miss Sometimes you are lucky but you don't want to have to rely on luck when it comes to dating. You want to make the best decision for yourself and not have it happen by chance. That's not to say that some happy accidents cannot occur, and you should be open to those, but what I am saying is that you are better off making an informed decision before just jumping in. Get to know him, his friends, a little about his history with women first. Has he had lots of three-month relationships and nothing long-term? That should tell you something. Is he a germ-a-phobe? Does he have other "issues" that you may not want to deal with? This is what dating is all about: learning about someone before deciding to make him yours. Also, look at the *real* him; be with him because he's a great guy, not because you've attached traits to him that aren't really there.

Mostly b's: On the money It helps that you're not high maintenance, but more important is that you know what you'll stand for and what you won't. When you first start dating someone, your instincts are good and you can tell if it will work or not. Just be aware that some guys are not always as they appear at first. Some will disguise a mean spirit with humor, while a really great guy may be hiding behind a shy exterior that you interpret as snobby. If you're too quick to judge you may let a really yummy guy slide through your fingers and wonder why there are no good guys around. Also keep in mind that being good at choosing guys doesn't mean that you are good at keeping them. If you find a really terrific guy, remember that you have to be a really terrific girl.

Mostly c's: Never know When a guy treats you like gold, you invest in silver; when he tells you that it's over, you camp out on his doorstep. You let the good ones get away and the bad ones rule your life. It's time to change that old pattern by thinking about what you want before you even get involved. You are someone who really needs a serious Essentials List. You also need to get your prior ties straight and make sure that on that list are things like ability to be close with you, and honest. This is important because you may have learned in the past not to trust men, so a great guy comes along and you don't trust him. If he has nothing to hide, please see that and know that not all guys are looking to hurt you. Someone wonderful will actually be wonderful if you let him. And remember, be realistic—Brad Pitt is never going to date you, but that doesn't mean that you don't get to be happy. You do!

thirty-six years old and a marketing associate for a top-of-the-line, well-known handbag company. She looks very young for her age, and meets lots of younger men as a result. This is especially the case for her in business because, as a marketing person, she is very involved with promotions (read: parties). The last three guys Caroline dated were:

- ◆ Mark, 22, a law student, for a year
- ◆ Alexander, 26, a graphic designer at his own start-up company, for eight months
- ◆ Gregory, 28, who just went back to school to get his M.B.A.; they were together almost two years

Caroline says that she cannot relate to men her own age and says that since she looks younger than she is and has such a young spirit, she doesn't see being happy with someone her own age, or heaven forbid, older. Her young looks aren't the only things that attract younger men to her; she is also relatively immature. Caroline swears that the problem with men who are in their late thirties is that they are all divorced, desperate, boring, or have some other lame quality, and she just doesn't want anything to do with them.

This is not to say that age matters in the long run, because it doesn't. Some very happy couples in very healthy relationships have age differences of ten years or more. In fact, when defending her penchant for younger men, Caroline usually references one of the happiest couples she knows, John and Kathy. Kathy is twelve years her husband's senior, and for them, it's utter bliss. Then again, that is the exception rather than the rule.

Another big factor in Caroline's previous relationships is that in each situation she was the person in control, and that's how Caroline would like to keep it. She likes being the one making the big bucks, as well as the major decisions in the relationship. While she doesn't need to date a guy who makes lots of cash, she would like to date one who feels secure in his career. According to Caroline, one of her attractions to younger men is that they look up to her and her professional accomplishments, and this gives her a sense of empowerment. Caroline has feminist ideals, and worries that a man her age would be less supportive of her liberal views. While this seems like the perfect premise for Caroline, in the end, however, it's always her Younger Guy boyfriends who break up with her. Usually this is because she wants to take the relationship to the next level emotionally, and they are simply not there yet.

In addition to being ready for an emotionally mature, serious relationship, Caroline also realizes that she really wants to get married and have children. And with her age approaching forty . . . tick, tick . . . she is starting to feel concerned that if she doesn't meet the right guy soon, she will be too late on the biological clock issue. So, in the interest of being specific and addressing all of her issues, Caroline needs to put on her list not just age appropriateness, but *life* appropriateness. Statistically, she may not find a twenty-six-year-old guy who is ready to settle down, get married, and start a family. Not many man muffins in their mid-twenties are both emotionally and financially prepared to take on that task. Though Caroline doesn't care about the financial part, that emotional part is key.

ESSENTIALS #1

It is not impossible that Caroline might meet a twenty-six-year-old who is in the same place as she is, but frankly, it's not likely. So, the first thing on Caroline's list must be:

1. *Age/life appropriateness: he must be in a place similar to where I am.* This is a compromise for Caroline, since she is a little bit of an ageist. However, who's to say that a man just a few years younger than she is, rather than seven or eight years younger, wouldn't be ready, willing, and able to take on the task of being everything Caroline wants? She doesn't have to go after men over forty if she isn't comfortable with them, but what about those in their early thirties? This leads us right into Caroline's next issue.

ESSENTIALS #2 AND #3

The second thing Caroline has to consider is that she keeps dating men who are at the beginning of their careers, and still have goals to reach that might be compromised if they were tied to a wife and children. What man, no matter how old he is, will be thinking about settling down when is just going back to school or is in his first significant job? So the *next* thing on Caroline's list should be the *nest* thing, meaning:

2. *He must be ready to think about a future with me (i.e., family, marriage etc.)* Another aspect of this that Caroline may not be considering has to do with the changing financial expectations of women and men in our society. Some men don't mind when a woman makes more money than they do; in fact, they like it! (And thank goodness for that, otherwise I would never have dated.) Let's call it the "Reese-and-Ryan Syndrome": the man has a fabulous career, the woman (Reese Witherspoon in this case) has a *way* more fabulous career, and both parties are okay with this. Many women live life by the Reese-and-Ryan Syndrome. It gives them the luxury of not feeling bad about being successful, unlike so many women before them, who have negotiated this kind of relationship in less liberated times. Living with a self-imposed glass ceiling would be insufferable for some women, and luckily, in this day and age, many men are happy to be the primary caregiver to their children. If no children are involved, this sort of man is happy to support his partner's life, and is not threatened by his partner's success. This kind of acceptance shows a special kind of love, but again, this reversal of traditional social roles is not for everyone.

Despite Caroline's professional success, she always ends up dating men who still like to be in that old-fashioned, stereotypical male role of "breadwinner" or "bring-home-the-bacon guy." What Caroline needs, though, is the exact opposite; she needs a guy who is 100 percent cool with her success and her financial status, and can go with the flow as far as her career is concerned. So, next on Caroline's list needs to be:

3. *I must stop dating the "I will take care of you when you quit your job" guy.* If Caroline waits for any of these Younger Guys she dates to get to that level in their careers, she might as well cross "kids" off her list of things to do before she dies, and just write "cats."

ESSENTIALS #4

Caroline's other issue is that her job is very demanding; it's a day job that occasionally turns into a night job. She may have a product-launch party at night, or a store opening in another city to which she will have to travel. Though she can occasionally bring a date along to events, most of the time she is working and needs to attend alone so as to remain focused. Some of Caroline's younger boyfriends of the past have been slightly too "oh-my-God-call-the-police" threatened by her job on two levels. One reason is that she is a real adult, doing real adult stuff that includes a huge amount of responsibility. Many younger guys have never encountered anyone in such a position before, aside from people their parents' age. While Caroline may feel like a twenty-two-year-old, the truth is, she isn't. She has to make sure everything goes smoothly at her events and even more important, she has to cultivate good working relationships with her business associates. The second reason that Caroline's boyfriends of the past have been threatened by her job is that sometimes those business associates whom she must work so hard to schmooze and impress happen to be men. Some of her exes have had a real problem with this: They didn't like her being at parties without them, nor did they enjoy her talking to other men, period. Now, this is not really an age issue as much as it is an emotional stability and insecurity issue. So, next on Caroline's list needs to be:

4. *He is totally secure with our relationship and trusts me.*

ESSENTIALS #5

The next thing Caroline mentioned was that when she had the "do you think you'll want kids one day" conversation with her boyfriend of two years, Gregory, he said that he was not sure, and it was a very uncomfortable conversation. She agonized about how to approach the subject with him at all, because she felt that Gregory was just *so completely* not in that place in his life that she couldn't even broach the topic with him. Then, when she finally worked up the courage to get the conversation going, he simply said he was "not sure." Caroline considers motherhood one of the most important parts of being a woman. She wants kids desperately and would even consider adopting or having a child on her own if she doesn't meet the right guy, which only illustrates how strongly she feels on the subject. So, next on her list must be:

5. *He has to want kids.*

ESSENTIALS #6

Let's face it, for Caroline, a shared desire to raise a family is essential! But there is something else that Caroline can extrapolate from her inability to broach the subject of kids with Gregory:

6. *He should be my best friend, and I should be able to talk to him about anything, without feeling judged.*

ESSENTIALS #7

The last thing item that Caroline put on her list is something that she didn't even realize was a dealbreaker for her until Gregory announced that he was getting his M.B.A. Caroline lives in Chicago and Gregory got into school in North Carolina, where he grew up. When he asked her to move there with him she realized that being in Chicago was important to her. She liked the big-city lifestyle, and all of her family lives in or around the city, which would be especially desirable to her once she had children.

Caroline has dreams of raising her children in close proximity to their cousins, grandparents, aunts, and uncles, not to mention a personal desire to be near her emotionally supportive family. There was no question in Caroline's mind that she would not be leaving the city that she loves, the city where she has worked so hard to establish her career. So, the last thing on Caroline's list was:

7. *He should either already live in or be willing to move to the Chicago area.* To some women, this would be a crazy demand, but it's a perfect example of how personal the Essentials List is. Caroline would never be happy outside of Chicago, away from her life and her family, so for her, it's a dealbreaker.

Elizabeth's Story

Meet Elizabeth, who is forty-two and works as a counselor at a youth center, where she runs the afterschool programs for the community. Elizabeth's loving nature is an asset in her work—and a liability in dating. Her penchant for helping troubled souls makes her vulnerable to both Wounded Guys and Party Guys, since she spends much of her time working with drug-addicted kids. Elizabeth's last three boyfriends were:

◆ Michael, a recovering heroin addict, for six years
◆ Ivan, an alcoholic, for about a year
◆ Max, a gambling addict, for three years

Elizabeth is another good example for you to consider. She always felt that her life, job, and upbringing were solid but a tad boring, so she decided to express her wild-child side in her dating

if you're trying to decide if he is right for you,
·· why don't you . . . ··

1. *Get the buzz on him:* Discreetly ask around about him. Someone you know always has the dish and is, of course, willing to tell all!

2. *Let the buyer beware:* You don't buy a dress without trying it on, so don't make a guy your one and only before he's had a chance to prove to you that he's as wonderful as you'd hoped.

3. *Decide before you meet him:* Use your Essentials List to figure out what *you* want ahead of time, so you can go into it with a clear head.

4. *Follow your gut:* If something tells you that he's *not* The One, trust your instincts. Your gut doesn't rationalize; your head does. Follow your gut if you want the truth of the matter.

5. *Don't ask, don't tell:* It's okay to go on a date and ask lots of questions; if you don't ask, you won't know. While you don't want it to be like a job interview, there are ways to ask questions without being so obvious. For example, if you want to know whether he dates a lot, you can certainly make a joke about how many girls he has taken to this restaurant, or you can disclose something about yourself that you really want to know about him. You can say, "You know, I like a beer or two after work, or sometimes wine with dinner, but I've never really been a big drinker." This may get him to tell you how much partying he does.

life. She lived up to that goal tenfold. Elizabeth was in a relationship for six years with Michael, who was a recovering heroin addict. He tried to go to Narcotics Anonymous meetings when he could, but like all programs that practice the "one size fits all" mentality of healing, it didn't work. She was instrumental in getting him into counseling, where he discovered that he was not healthy enough to be in a relationship. He subsequently ended his relationship with Elizabeth.

After Michael, Elizabeth dated guys who on the surface seemed like "nice" guys, but always had a secret darkness to their personalities. Elizabeth's favorite boyfriend, Ivan, was a Party Guy for sure. She knew him from a Mexican-themed bar she would sometimes go to for margarita happy hours after work with her coworkers. She would see him there regularly, and one day he struck up a conversation with Elizabeth. He was dark skinned, had a great sense of humor, and she found him to be sexy as hell. *Ivan the terrible*, she thought to herself. It wasn't until a few weeks into the relationship that she realized his Party Guy ways were really an issue. Ivan wasn't just an "after-work-margarita guy"—he had a serious drinking problem. When he was drunk, she saw a total personality shift: he really *was* "Ivan the terrible." At first Elizabeth hoped that she could help Ivan, maybe get him counseling as she did with Michael. But Ivan liked drinking; he enjoyed it and didn't want to change his ways. Eventually, they broke up.

After Ivan, Elizabeth dated a succession of more innocuous Party Guys; nothing like Ivan the Terrible, just daily-pot-smoker kinds of men. Then she met Max at a party he was throwing after a big-money win in Las Vegas, to which she was invited by a girlfriend.

ESSENTIALS #1

At the party Elizabeth noticed that Max wasn't drinking or smoking or anything, and through her conversation with him, she learned he was a religious man. Max was sweet, cute, and by some miracle, single. Elizabeth had decided that her dealbreaker numero uno should be:

1. *Can no longer date guys with drug or alcohol problem.* In light of his behavior at the party, Max seemed to be a good candidate. Elizabeth and Max had a wonderful first month. Max was a sports fanatic, so he took her to football games, basketball games, even to a women's professional soccer game. She thought it was just his idea of a fun night out, until she noticed that for each of the games they attended, he had football and basketball pools going, at the same time. He even was betting on the women's soccer game! She noticed the same mood and personality change in him when he lost as she did with her drunk and drug-addicted Party Guy exes.

ESSENTIALS #2

Elizabeth was devastated to realize that Max was a gambler. How was it possible that she hooked up with another addict? She'd already hidden car keys when she was with Ivan, threatened to leave when she was with Michael, and arranged more than one intervention in her lifetime. She had really thought that she was done with all of that. So, now Elizabeth had another principle to add to her list:

2. *No longer date men that need to be fixed.*

ESSENTIALS #3 AND #4

Elizabeth's specificity didn't end there. She had a revelation when she broke up with Max, and decided that she no longer wanted to keep making the same mistakes over and over. Somehow Elizabeth had been dating the same men in different packages, and now that she was over forty, something had to change. That meant that an overhaul of her dating perspective needed to occur. Her list needed to include more than just "No longer date men that need to be fixed." The next two items on her list read like this:

3. *Only go after men who are worthy of my love and attention.*
4. *Recognize that I am deserving of being loved back as good as I give, so he needs to love me . . . a lot.*

ESSENTIALS #5

Elizabeth also realized that by dating damaged men who needed to be fixed by her, the relationship became all about them and her needs were seldom met. So next on her list she wrote:

5. *Thinks my needs are important and is not just willing but eager to make me happy.*

ESSENTIALS #6

Finally, Elizabeth put something very simple on her list, something she took a long time to discover. This was something real and central for her to have in a relationship:

6. *He gets me.* During her dating overhaul, it occurred to Elizabeth that she never knew how any of her boyfriends really felt

about her. Did they see that she was an amazing woman that they were lucky to have? Her guess was: probably not. They didn't appreciate her, and they didn't get her. When she looked at herself through their eyes, it wasn't pleasant. She saw herself as a woman who tolerated situations that did not make her happy, with men who did not truly care about her, and who certainly didn't get her.

Felicia's Story

Meet Felicia, age thirty-four, who is a lawyer and, sadly, hates her job. Felicia became a lawyer because her mother was one, and since she really didn't have any direction in her life, she went to law school because she could. In the past she had been treated terribly in relationships. She was married for a short time, but soon divorced after she found out that her husband had cheated on her. Felicia's most recent dating history includes:

- Roger, the Party Guy, who she dated for two years
- Leo, the Workout Guy, who she was with for over a year
- Nick, the Wounded Guy, who she dated for six months
- Carlos, the Older Guy, who she was with for eight months

Felicia's divorce left her seriously bitter, and very mistrustful of men. Her demeanor when she went out on dates, or even just out to meet new men, was both aggressive and jaded. Felicia's friends weren't sure if she even realized how she came across, but they figured that she had been hurt enough, and they didn't want to be the ones to tell her that her behavior was most likely sabotaging her dating potential. They hoped that she would just grow out of it. Felicia's friends saw her repeating a depressing pattern that turned her negative opinions of men in general into a self-fulfilling prophecy. She would date the wrong guys and then wonder why they didn't call her. Her friends tried to tell her that she didn't really want these guys to call, "good riddance to bad rubbish,'" and all that. Nevertheless, Felicia kept dating men who provided her with a continual stream of proof that men are scum. She kept the cycle going all by herself, despite her friends' best efforts to guide her toward better men. Felicia believed that men were awful, and she always found men who supported her belief system. Roger, the Party Guy, said that going out with Felicia was like being on a job interview. She barely cracked a smile and kept asking him question after question, as though she were reading them from cue cards. Not that Roger was good for her anyway, but here she was, purposely choosing the wrong guy, and then pushing him away before he even had a chance to prove himself otherwise. At least, in the case of Roger, Felicia was pushing him in the right direction. In order to relieve some stress at work, Felicia started taking karate lessons on Tuesday and Thursday nights, where she hooked up with Leo, one of the instructors. Leo was the Workout Guy, mixed with a touch of the Proximity Guy, as he was simultaneously dating another girl in the Monday and Wednesday class, as well as the owners' daughter. Felicia broke it off with Leo as soon as she found this out. "See, men are scum!" she exclaimed.

The most awful of Felicia's dating duds, though, was Nick, the Wounded Guy, who had gotten out of his divorce less than a month before they met. Nick says that Felicia showed up on their first date demanding to know what "the plan" was, and when he said he didn't have one, she said, "Let's not play games, shall we, let's just go to dinner." Felicia came across like she just wanted a free meal, or went out just so she didn't have to stay home by herself that evening. Nick stayed with her because she had already been through a divorce and he needed a sounding board as he struggled through the breakup of his own marriage. Plus, they dished about what jerks their exes had been together, which was a little morbid, but kind of fun. Felicia couldn't wait to get that relationship over with so she could include Nick on her list as another guy who didn't like her and wasn't very nice to her. It encouraged and reinforced her negativity.

Finally, Felicia turned to Internet dating on a site for divorcées. She began a series of e-mail relationships, one in particular with an Older Guy named Carlos. Felicia was way into Carlos, and would run home from work and go straight to her computer to see if Carlos had written her. Before she knew it, she was pouring her heart out to this virtual stranger. Her daily musings to him were less an e-mail chain and more of a diary. Felicia opened up to him about everything that she was feeling, and he responded in kind. Carlos was warm and honest: they talked about their exes, their dreams, their futures, and they commiserated about work, life, and the things that got them down, too. One side of Felicia was a little embarrassed at how open she had been with Carlos, but another part of her was proud that she had finally managed to meet someone who didn't seem to be "scum." Carlos said that he wanted to make plans to come see her, but every time they tried to get together, something would come up. Months went by and Carlos never made the plan. It soon became clear why: One day Felicia received an e-mail from a woman named Ingrid, Carlos's wife. The "ex" that Carlos had mentioned in his daily musings was not an ex at all. Felicia was devastated that, once again, she had opened herself up and gotten hurt. She soon stopped going to the chat rooms and took herself off the Internet dating site altogether.

There Felicia was, back in her apartment on a Saturday night, vowing never to get involved with a man again. Felicia was all dated out. Her friends felt for her, and were hopeful that she would seek help, perhaps go to therapy and deal with some of her anger. Eventually, she did. Then, she sat down with me and made her Essentials List.

ESSENTIALS #1

Given that Felicia had been hurt a number of times in her previous relationships, trust was extremely high on her priority list. But Felicia also knew there were several aspects to the trust issue that needed to be included in her most perfect relationship. So, first on her list was:

1. *I have to be able to trust him completely.*

ESSENTIALS #2

Part and parcel of being able to trust a man completely for Felicia was:

2. *I need to be with a person who is completely honest and open about every aspect of his life.* While Felicia wasn't trying to control a man, or keep her finger on his pulse all day, she knew she wanted to be with someone who actually had nothing to hide. If she could believe in this, she would be able to build up her trust in men again.

ESSENTIALS #3 AND #4

Felicia also learned during the course of her dating misadventures that e-mail relationships are a perfect way to invent the person you are dating. When communicating through e-mail, you don't get to see how a person is listening to you, or even if he is listening to you at all. Conveniently, you can fabricate half of his personality. Felicia had created Carlos in her mind as a wonderful, trustworthy guy, which he clearly was not. After pouring her heart out to this virtual stranger, she was so vulnerable, she was willing to believe anything he said. So, the next two items on her list were:

3. *No more e-mail relationships. If I do meet someone online, I will get to know him in person and not over e-mail.*

4. *Since I'm still vulnerable, I need to be with someone who is willing to get to know me slowly.*

ESSENTIALS #5 AND #6

Next, Felicia recognized that she would consistently choose men who were not right for her because she truly wanted to believe that "men are scum." Now she had to try to undo her usual pattern. Although Felicia did select men who were either too broken to focus on her needs or too self-involved to be a healthy half of a relationship, she decided to add:

5. *I need a man who has come to terms with his own issues and has a way to deal with problems as they arise with me.*

6. *I need a man who can make me a priority. Someone who will make me feel that I am important too.*

ESSENTIALS #7

Felicia also became aware that one of the main aspects of a relationship that she was missing, one that she felt would make the difference, was this:

7. *I need to be with someone who is committed to making a relationship happen with me.* She saw that the common thread in all her previously failed relationships was the lack of commitment to do whatever it takes to make it work.

ESSENTIALS #8

Last, Felicia, at thirty-four, felt the pressure to be in a relationship before she was forty. Well, these days, what the heck is forty? Nothing, that's what. Women are under no pressure to do anything by any age. We are living longer, healthier lives and if we want to have children later in life, we can adopt or go through in vitro fertilization. There are no more limits on us other than those that we have imposed on ourselves. Usually Felicia rushed into things with guys too quickly because of this age pressure, and she realized that she had to take anxiety about age out of the equation; otherwise, she knew would end up settling for less than she deserved in a man. So her final item became:

8. *Forty is just a number, and don't go out with just anyone out of fear of forty.* By lightening up about age, Felicia freed herself to meet men who *really* wanted to get to know her. This also allows her ample time to really get to know a guy before deciding to give her heart. So what that she's almost forty? Forty is the new thirty, you know!

With her Essentials List in place, Felicia felt more confident to begin dating again. Her newfound confidence, coupled with therapy to deal with her anger issues, made Felicia feel that she was now ready to be the best "other half" of a relationship that she could be. She was empowered and optimistic again, a perfect attitude to have as she dives back into the dating pool.

chapter eleven

your essentials list: the workbook

The question now is, how do you start to put your Essentials List together? Let's get down to business. In the grand scheme of things, it's not really important why you dated each one of those guys. What is important is that you are no longer dating them, and that you are ready to be with The One, your Mr. Right. Those ridiculous guys and all of the game-playing and public embarrassments that go along with them seem to be far behind you. But are they really?

Maybe we should take a step back and explore why a perfectly sane woman would date, and even perhaps think about being serious with, any of the guys loitering in the first half of this book. Until you get a handle on why you dated them, you will not be able to assess why you shouldn't date them, and you will have a hard time moving on and recognizing The One when he shows up.

Before we get started, it's important to lay down a few ground rules, which I urge you not to break!

Ground Rules

Rule #1: I will accept and move on

Remember, life is about making good choices for yourself. Learning to make good choices comes from making bad choices, so don't chastise yourself for dating the wrong guys in the first place. It's a good thing that you dated the bad ones, because now you have a blueprint for what didn't work. Within that blueprint are the answers to the question, "What is my Essentials List going to look like?" You can spend all of your time lamenting about what worked and what didn't, but I don't want you to lament; I want you to learn. Time heals nothing. It is what you do in that time that will make the difference.

Rule #2: I will NOT try to get him back

The secret to finding the right guy for you is actually not a secret at all. You already have all of the information that you need to figure out what kind of guy is right; you just need to access it. First of all, you have to put aside any thoughts that would be considered self-sabotage. Those are the thoughts that ask endless questions about why your last relationship didn't work out. You have to stop asking those questions with the purpose of trying to figure out how to get him back. Instead, ask them with the purpose of finding a true understanding of why you made the choices you did. If your intention is to try to revisit a bad romance with someone who was actually wrong for you, you have to stop doing that right now. Stop, seriously—otherwise I'm not going to tell you how to find a great guy.

Okay, now, first things first—we are trying to get you to move on. This means dropping all questions that deal with trying to figure out who he is, why he does what he does, and why he treated you like he did, because the answer should always be WHO CARES? This is about you, not him. Don't try to analyze him; he can get his own book for that. Let's focus on you and why you do what *you* do. Keeping that focus is a much more important step in helping you move toward the right guy. To make the best Essentials List, you need to decide what you want, but you need to do that almost in a vacuum. In other words, if you have someone in mind at the moment, forget about him, even if it's just someone you saw on a bus and fantasized about, creating a whole perfect life together in your mind. This also includes someone with whom you've had a couple of dates, and as a result are feeling wildly optimistic. Drop it now, because it will confound your thoughts. You need to be clean-slate girl—Tabula Rasa. Simply put, you have to pretend "he" doesn't exist. This is especially true if you just got out of something heavy. You have to picture your life *before* you even met him. If you can't do that, then maybe you can drop something heavy on your head so we can start fresh, okay?

Rule #3: I will be completely objective

The reason for this rule is that you *must* be objective and you *need* to be objective in order to put together a list that will really help you change things and stop making the same mistakes. If you can't do this, you may find a way to work one of Mr. Wrong's qualities into the Essentials List, one of his negative qualities that you didn't like in the first place, and then you are back to square one. This has to be about what you really want. For example, perhaps somewhere in your mind, you've always known that

···· listen up ·····

Some brilliant scholars have found that what you are really thinking about in your relationships is apparent in your conversation. Listen to what your date is saying too when you are out with him; he will tell you what he is looking for. You just have to learn to pay attention. Let's say that you are out with a perfectly normal, seemingly charming potential cuddle bunny and he is talking about his future, which involves scaling the Andes, skydiving into volcanoes, and whitewater rafting down the Amazon. First you think adventure guy sounds like he is still searching for the fountain of youth, a soul, whatever. You may see his freewheeling life as meaning he's not ready to settle down. Then he says that an adventure isn't worth having unless you share it with someone special. Hmmmmm, good words to hear. Okay, he wants a relationship. Score one for his side.

This same kind of interpretation works for you, too; remember this advice when you are out on a date with someone, and find yourself talking about your career and all of the ins and outs of your job. He may see that as *you* not wanting to settle down. You can be career-focused, but you also have to be a good date. You may have tried to play it cool, and by doing that turned off a great guy who could have been your destiny.

And ladies, *please* keep this rule in mind when you are dating a guy who really likes you but tells you that he is not looking for anything serious. You may think, "Nah, he can't mean that. When he falls for me, he'll feel differently." I'm not saying that it *never* happens, but it's not likely. The man is telling you what he doesn't want, and you have to learn to listen to his words.

you need a guy who can let stuff roll off his back, and doesn't take life too seriously. You aren't an uptight person, you are a California-style laid-back chick, and you don't get too upset about things. Now let's say that the last guy who knocked your socks off happened to be a bit too serious, and you compromised that quality, even though deep-down inside, it drove you nuts. Whenever someone shortchanged him at a store or cut him off in traffic, he was a ball of stress waiting to explode, and sometimes maybe he did explode, irrationally. It was one of his qualities that you really hated, but you told yourself you could tolerate it because he had other good qualities.

Well, to make the best list for yourself, you have to recognize your original desire to be with a guy who is not too serious and can take things in stride. It is indeed essential to you. The idea of this list is that you don't have to compromise. You are creating the perfect guy for yourself in this list. Then as soon as you know what qualities that perfect guy for you has, you'll recognize him when you meet him. Notice that I am saying the perfect guy "for you." It's not about a perfect guy in general, because we all know that's not possible. You may like a laid-back guy, but your sister may not care about that sort of thing; she is really looking for someone who doesn't want kids. "For you": I cannot stress that enough, the idea of individuality and how that will be reflected in your Essentials List.

How to Figure Out Your Essentials

Let's get started, shall we? The first step toward making your Essentials List is to take a close look at your past relationships.

Why didn't they work? What were the dealbreakers that caused the relationship to end each time? Who ended it? Each experience will offer enough information for us to figure out exactly what should be on your list. So grab a pen and paper; we're actually going to spell out what ended your relationship. Be honest about it—otherwise this exercise is not going to help you. Here's a quick example, to give you an idea of how to go about this.

julie's
····· essentials list ························

My last relationship broke up because: "I admit that maybe I was a bit lonely when I met Ricardo. All of my friends were dating someone, and I was sick of having nothing to do on a Saturday night. Ricardo was very sweet and he liked me and honestly, I could have done worse. Anyway, things were great at first, but as the relationship went on, there were so many things about him that drove me crazy. He seemed really focused on his career, and totally uninterested in making me a priority. We used to fight about that all the time. He broke up with me, actually, but I think I kinda drove him to it. I was on him all the time about working late and not thinking about my needs. It wasn't like he had women throwing themselves at him. He was lucky to have me, and he even told me that at first. By the time we broke it off, though, I think he was just sick of me yelling at him all the time. It got really frustrating. I would yell at him to be with me and it totally made him not want to be with me. He broke it off, but it was totally my fault."

It's pretty clear from her story that one of Julie's Essentials should be: He has to make her a priority. Julie needs to feel that, even if her guy's career is important to him, she is too. Julie needs to be with a guy who can handle both her needs and the needs of his job. If Ricardo could have done this in the first place, she never would have been yelling at him about it. Another issue is to note is that Julie admittedly dated Ricardo out of loneliness and boredom. Now, there's nothing wrong with that, as long as you recognize this when you are doing it. You have got to say to yourself, "I'm bored, and this guy is fine till my soul mate comes along." It's a mistake to try to make something work when you know from the beginning it's the wrong relationship. So also on Julie's list should be: Do not make a stopover a long-term thing. It's either there or it's not with a guy. Don't fool yourself into trying to make some-thing fit that you *know* does not, especially if you knew it from the beginning. Heck, even if you live in a town with twelve people and you've dated all of them, there's always the Internet. There are men everywhere these days, so the excuse of settling for less than what you really want is no longer an option.

First Things First

Okay, let's do step number one together. This is where you take a fine-tooth comb to your past relationships and really assess why they didn't work. Put down the reasons he gave, the reasons you gave, and what you really think happened. You might even want to include what attracted you to him in the first place. Sometimes that, in and of itself, will tell you why it didn't work. Was he a rebound? Were you experimenting with Proximity Guy, or was he your first Younger Guy and you were dying to see what all the fuss was about? (Thanks for nothing, Demi!)

My last relationship broke up because:

_____

_____

_____

The relationship before that broke up because:

_____

_____

_____

Another long-term relationship that I thought would last broke up because:

_____

_____

_____

Yet another long-term relationship that I thought would last broke up because:

_____

_____

_____

What Your Answers Say about Your Essentials List

Let's have a general discussion about some of the most common reasons that women give when asked why a relationship didn't work. Then you can see if they correspond to anything you might have thought or may have even written down.

> *Reason: "We broke up because I wanted to take it to the next level and he did not."—Candace*
>
> Maybe Candace's ex wanted to go to grad school, take a job across the country, date other women, who knows? Whatever details caused the breakdown of her last relationship are irrelevant, because the core of it all is that she was ready to take it further, and he was not. Sound familiar? If so, this should lead you to the conclusion that the two of you were in different places in your lives, and were just not right for each other. So, your Essentials List should include something like this: "He is looking for a long-term relationship."

> *Reason: "We were always fighting."—Naomi*
>
> This is a tricky one, and if you wrote down something similar to this, you'll need to go deeper than that to figure out *why* you guys were fighting. Was it over money? If so, then maybe you need to be with someone who has the same philosophy about money that you do. If you are into saving money to the point where overspending, or even day-to-day spending, gives you too much anxiety, then you should absolutely consider that for your list. Or maybe your money issue is that you like to spend whatever you have, and enjoy your life. If that's how you like to live, then you need to be with someone who shares that philosophy. It's not about

money, really; it's about being of the same mind with respect to a major life issue. (One that tends to break up marriages.) The idea is that you and he need to be on the same page. If you fought about money, then chances are that you did not have the same attitude about it. Money issues between couples exist no matter how much you have. Most of the time, money equals caring in people's minds, and the amount of money you spend and the things you spend it on is symbolic in some way of how you feel about each other. Money can be used as a way to express unexpressed emotions between you and your sweetie. Hence, if money was the issue, you really need to narrow down why: What did it represent? What did it symbolize? Put words to the feelings, and then put those words on the list!

If, on the other hand, you were always fighting about aspects of his personality that drove you crazy, which ones were they? Was he too career-oriented for you, or not enough? Was he insensitive to your feelings, or too sensitive and easily hurt by you? If you and your ex fought all the time, ask yourself if you were mad because he wasn't what you were looking for, or if there were real issues there. If the answer is that you resented him for not being The One, that isn't his fault; it's yours for settling for less than you wanted. You were angry with him for being him. It's not his fault that he didn't measure up to what you needed. Again, why you fought is the most important thing to understand. It will provide insight into which qualities need to be on your list.

Reason: "We broke up because I just didn't love him anymore." —Bernadette

Hello! Of course this is a valid reason to get out of a relationship, but if you don't understand why you fell out of love with

it's not just
a girl thing

Good news, girls! A whole new phenomenon is going on! According to relationship experts, women are no longer more relationship-oriented than men. In fact, from one day to the next, men are more consistent with that desire for a future than we are. Men, more than women, have come to the conclusion that real happiness comes from having good relationships and not from bedding as many babes as possible and making millions of dollars. The guys are catching on! Can I get a "woo hoo"? That also means that men have a more consistent idea of what they are looking for, and are much better at systematically making it happen. That's the point of the Essentials List: knowing what you want and going after it. The research shows that men have already got that down, so it's time that we went out and did the same.

him, it isn't going to help you much. What was it about him that couldn't sustain your affections long-term? Was he not exciting enough? Was it hot and heavy in the beginning, but then, when the smoke cleared, he wasn't what you had expected? When Seema first met Nathaniel it was at a fundraiser for a charity that she deeply believed in. The night was a whirlwind; he donated a great deal of money, they had a great time at the silent auction, and they talked till three in the morning. One night about six months into the relationship, he leaned over to kiss her and she was completely repulsed. "It was like kissing my brother," Seema

·· fight right ··

Fighting can actually be quite a healthy thing in a relationship. Did you know that there are four factors that can help you be a rational thinker during a fight? Keeping these in mind will steer you away from getting needlessly knee-deep into a fight, and bring you in to a more understanding place, so that you can see what's really going on when you argue with your man.

1. *Don't exaggerate.* Sometimes when emotions are running high, especially an emotion like anger, your judgments can be clouded. If you can try to avoid the tendency to exaggerate and focus on the negative, that will be your first step in getting through the fight.

2. *This is not a hostage situation.* You have to find a way to not demand that your wishes should always be met. It is fine to ask for what you need, but remember that demanding and deserving are two separate things.

3. *Avoid statements like* "You *always . . .* " or "We *never . . .* " The final tactic that many people employ during an argument is to globally rate a situation or a *relationship.* When you do that it closes the possibility that the situation can ever change. You are accepting it as a *fête accompli.*

4. *Keep your eye on the prize.* Remember that you love him and that he is not your enemy, nor is he a previous boyfriend who wronged you or a parent who treated you unfairly. Don't make him pay for their mistakes. He is the man in your life and ultimately, while you do want to get your point across, you don't want to alienate him.

says. "I couldn't stand him and I did not see it coming." Seema later figured out that during the relationship she began to feel that she did not respect him. It was a slow burn, but it culminated that night with the kiss. Nathaniel was a very weak-willed man. He made very few decisions for himself, which at first Seema thought was the good kind of vulnerable, until that moment of the kiss. It seemed that she stopped loving him all in that moment, but really, it was a long time coming. Seema needs a stronger man, one who is decisive and not "wimpy," as she put it. So on her list (which again, might not be on yours) is: "He needs to be a strong decision-making type."

Reason: "He had too many problems that I couldn't fix by myself, that's why I ended it."—Pat

Well, of course, all relationships have issues, and all people have problems. Finding your Mr. Right is just a matter of deciding what you are willing to work through with your sweetie, and knowing when to call it quits if he isn't willing to work with you. If his father was abusive, for example, he may have some degree of emotional baggage that he brings with him to the relationship. If he isn't willing to work through the damage he sustained because of it, though, how can you be expected to solve this problem alone? If his first marriage ended because his wife cheated on him, and he has serious trust issues that he doesn't acknowledge, then he isn't for you. To be in a healthy relationship, you have to both be able to put a mirror up for each other and clearly reflect who you both are. It's the only way to continue growing as individuals and as a couple. It is also the only way to stop repeating patterns.

The reward will be a great, close relationship with each other, and that should be essential to everyone's list: Two people who are willing to acknowledge the truths in their lives, and deal with them head-on together, with the ultimate goal of having an intimate and secure relationship.

Reason: "I was always walking on eggshells with him, nothing I did was ever good enough or right."—Helene

Hypercritical behavior is learned behavior, and usually pops up when someone has a parent who always made them feel that they were never good enough. Or, if you had a parent who made you feel that way, you could be sabotaging your relationship with your own self-critical behavior. On the other hand, he could also be a total control freak. If you are like Helene, and this was a major reason that your relationship broke up, you'll need to dissect it. In what aspects of your life did he make you feel like nothing was ever right or good enough? All aspects of your life, or just some areas? If this sounds like you, then you may want to consider adding an item to your Essentials List that says your guy cannot judge you and should embrace all aspects of your personality. Acceptance is really what we all desire most. Having something on your list who acknowledges this basic need could be a boon for your next relationship.

Reason: "My relationship ended when he cheated on me." —Rianna

Again, this is fair grounds for insta-breakup. However, if you don't examine your own behavior as it relates to his infidelity, you aren't going to learn anything from all that heartache. Just putting

"I need to trust him" on your Essentials List might not be enough. It would serve you better to figure out *why* he cheated. Was it because he knew that you weren't the one and he figured, why not? Was it because he was incredibly insecure and needed to feel attractive to as many women as he possibly could? If he cheated, it is important for you to understand why, so that you don't wind up with a guy who cheats on you again. Was it because he was immature, or because he was a sex addict? Those are two totally different concepts, and will give a very different shape to what you put on your list. Did you have a role in it? If so, what was it? Remember, it can be as simple as this: you picked the wrong guy.

The Plan

Okay, we've spent lots of time reviewing your history, asking tough questions, and thinking about what kinds of sins of the past you don't want to repeat in your future. Nice work, girl! Now, we need to discuss your plan for your future and do a little goal-setting. If you want a satisfying life, setting goals is one of the key strategies you can master right now to help yourself achieve it. First you have to think big: imagine your perfect life and your largest goal; what you want the most in your future. Then we'll set smaller goals that you can achieve, one by one, in service of your greater plan. A great way to illustrate this is with a conversation I had recently with Danielle about her future:

> *Danielle:* I really want to be famous. (Largest goal)
> *Me:* At what?

Danielle: I want to be a famous lawyer. (More specific)
Me: Well then, let's set some goals to get you there. First, have you gone to law school?
Danielle: No. (Going to law school, smaller goal)
Me: Well, have you applied?
Danielle: No.
Me: Have you taken the LSAT? (Smallest goal to get her to the next small goal, all in service of the largest goal, being a famous lawyer)
Danielle: No.
Me: Well, let's start there then.

It's really the same with dating. When I interviewed Kimberly for this book she kept saying, "I just want to be married." I asked her, "To whom?" She really had no one in particular in mind, so I asked her to take a step back, and start with a smaller goal, which for her was meeting someone she liked. Her first step was to make an Essentials List and decide exactly what she wanted in a guy. Next, she made it her mission to find someone she liked. Clearly this is no easy feat, and is the type of thing that could require time and patience, but within a year of our interview, Kimberly found Christopher.

So, remember, before you can say, "I just want to be married," a whole bunch of stuff needs to happen. It took Kimberly time to establish a bond with Christopher, but the next time I saw her, she had a much more realistic, achievable goal for herself. Instead of saying "I just want to be married," Kimberly now told me, "I want to marry *Christopher.*"

Now it's your turn.

<h3>what about</h3>

your friends?

As we move to new cities and away from our parents and siblings, our friends become our new families. As a result, we begin to parent each other. I cannot count how many times a friend has told me who I really am, or what I am doing wrong—probably more than my own mother did. As much as you hate to hear it when your friends shed light upon your less than desirable qualities, they are often right! Listening to them can be very cathartic. A friend may say, "You always go after guys who . . . " or "You never do . . . (this or that)." As much as you may not want to admit they are right, you have to at least examine what it is they are telling you. I had a friend once who said to me, "I don't have everything I want, but I seem to have a lot of the things that *you* want." This was a real eye-opener for both of us. It forced her to appreciate her life and in turn it forced me to contend with what it was that I was missing that she seemed to have. She forced me to look at patterns that I had, what worked and what didn't, so that I was able to put my list together.

Friends you have had your entire life are a great reality check. Maybe you can try talking to some of them about what you should look for in your perfect guy. They could be of some help because they know you very well. They also can say things like, "Sam was such a jerk but nobody wanted to upset you because you were so blinded by love," or "Michael was amazing, we couldn't believe you dumped him." Y'know, encouraging stuff like that.

In five years I see myself being . . .

The importance of having a plan is illustrated in this study: A few years back two researchers in New York, Peter Gollwitzer and Gabrielle Oettingen, asked a few hundred college students to write an essay over their Christmas holiday break about what Christmas means to them. Some of the students were asked specifically when they would be writing it. Those students had to give an exact time, place, or situation in which they would be writing their essay. Answers included "I'll write my essay Christmas morning right after opening gifts," or "I will write my essay before I leave for midnight mass," that kind of thing. The other students who participated were told to write it whenever they chose, and to just have it back to the researchers when they got back from vacation. What Gollwitzer and Oettingen found was that just about all of the students who made a specific plan as to when they would write their essays were the ones who actually wrote them. Furthermore, they wrote their essays exactly when they said they would. The other students, who had no plan but were just given a nebulous "finish it whenever," never turned in their essays. This is just one example of many studies that emphasize the need to have a plan, or a goal. So, let's set some goals, shall we? We're going to write a list of five things you would like to have if a fairy godmother appeared and offered to grant you five wishes. In five years I *would love to* see myself having:

1. _____

2. _____

3. _____

4. _____

5. _____

Okay, now we're going to plant our feet back on the ground and try this again, being totally realistic. In five years I *totally and realistically* see myself having:

1. _____

2. _____

3. _____

4. _____

5. _____

In ten years I see myself being . . .

Let's turn it up a notch. Armed with your five-year wish list and your five-year reality list, let's construct a ten-year plan. This time we're just going to do one plan, a realistic one, based on your previous two lists. What you might find is that some of the items on that fantasy list are things that you can actually do in ten years. In ten years I see myself:

1. _____

2. _____

3. _____

4. _____

5. _____

The secret to goal attainment, or reaching those goals on your list, is to set smaller goals that are related to the bigger goal. Research shows that personally valued, closer-to-home goals are not just easier to reach; it's also likely that you'll be far more motivated to achieve them. In other words, something that you think you are totally capable of accomplishing in your future will inspire in you the means to get there.

So, how do you work these five- and ten-year plans into your Essentials List? Let's take a look at how Carla did it. Carla is thirty-two years old and has been working as a dental hygienist for a few years now because it's a "good job" that pays her bills—but the reality is, she doesn't love it. What Carla really wants is a big life change: she wants a husband and she wants a new career. Before she and I set out to make her Essentials List, we sat down and discussed her five-year plan. Carla wanted to become a chef, she hoped to be married, and she decided that she wanted to be a mother, regardless of whether she was married or not. The first thing we did was to figure out how she can move from cleaning teeth to terrine of beef. She made the following lists:

carla's five-year plan . . .

in five years i see myself:

1. As a chef in a small restaurant
2. Making plans to open a restaurant (finding investors, etc.)
3. Married to a fabulous guy
4. Owning my own apartment
5. Starting a family

The first two goals were simple, really: Carla's larger goal was to be a chef, which motivated her to take the steps she needed. She figured time was going to pass if she was in school or not, so she went to culinary school at night to earn her hours and work her externship. At culinary school she decided she wanted to specialize in a gourmet version of Tex-Mex cooking, and decided that she was going to set her goal for master chef, the highest title you can achieve in a kitchen. After finishing up culinary school, she applied for line-cook jobs at local restaurants. She also got a gig writing a food review in her local paper, which she thought would give her the opportunity to network with restaurant owners and to see what kinds of restaurants were doing well in the area, what the emerging trends were, and so on.

Carla had no trouble meeting guys, and ended up dating one guy who was in her program at school, and another who was a sous-chef at the restaurant where she did her externship. It's been almost three years since we put Carla's five-year plan into action.

Now, let's take a look at Carla's Essentials List:

1. *I need to be with someone who is supportive of my career goals.* If I decide to change them again, I want to be with someone who can roll with it. Part of being flexible in the career department is that I need to be with a guy who is mobile. If I have a job opportunity at a restaurant in another city, I want him to be able to come with me. So, the whole career-supportive thing is a big one.

2. *I need to be with someone who wants children, or at least one child.* I was an only child and I'm cool with having just one, but I wouldn't mind not stopping there.

3. *I need to be with a guy who isn't a perfectionist.* I had a mother who was a total perfectionist. I put enough pressure on myself as a result of my upbringing, and need a laid-back kind of guy to balance me out.

4. *I need someone with a good sense of humor, even funny.* I get very uptight, and I *cannot* be with another type-A personality. He needs to balance out my intensity and make me laugh.

5. *I need to be with someone who will compromise and be really flexible with me.* My last boyfriend and another boyfriend I had a few years back were both *very* stubborn. It was the root of most of our issues, so much so that I realize now, it's a dealbreaker for me.

The last time I spoke with Carla, her sous-chef seemed to fit all of her list items, and their relationship was rapidly moving forward. They had even begun to discuss moving in together. The day that they did, he proposed. I wonder what I'll wear to the wedding?

the single girl's manifesto to finding her mr. right

Now let's write down your Essentials List. You should look at it as your list of demands. The idea is that you are unbending, as if you have taken your own social life hostage and if these demands are not met, you will not continue the relationship. This list should contain four to seven items, depending on you. But keep in mind, less than four may not really create a clear picture, and more than seven is just greedy, girlfriend! Your Essentials are:

1. _____

2. _____

3. _____

4. _____

5. _____

6. _____

7. _____

foolproofing your list

You've done a tremendous amount of work so far—getting your list started is half the battle. At this point, there may be some things on your Essentials List that are really not as important as you think. The topics we cover in this chapter will help you to shape and revise your list into the best possible list it can be before you go out into the dating world. Your power is in your own belief that what you need is in tune with what you want. Moreover, you need to understand what constitutes "nice-to-have" traits in your Mr. Right, and what should be defined as "imperative" ones. In this chapter, we're going to make sure that you're not missing some of the fundamentals that make a healthy relationship work. Without those on your list, you'll be back at square one, and will continue to make the same mistakes. We're going to give your list a quick once-over, just to make absolutely sure that you're good to go.

Cooper's Golden Rules

Maybe the concept of the Essentials List isn't totally new to you. First, if you have thought about this previously, and already made a sort of "list of rules" in your head before even picking up this book, good for you! Second, since your list hasn't worked thus far, let me suggest a few things that you should put on it. Let me also point out that if, at first glance, you don't think these items are important, you need to reexamine your Essentials List and give some thought to what you are really looking for. You see, the few items that I am about to add to your list are the cornerstones of good relationships. I didn't come up with these all by myself; these facts were learned from years and years of research conducted by many very talented and capable scientists. While I have said many times throughout this book that this list should be as incredibly individual as you are, there are a few truths as to why some relationships flourish while others crash and burn. We will consider these our three Golden Rules. Add one to your Essentials List, or all three—but ignore them at your peril!

The Communication Rule

It is imperative that your list contains something about communication, however you phrase it. Perhaps you said: "I have to be able to be honest with him about anything without the expectation of being judged," or maybe something like: "We should be best friends," meaning you tell each other everything and it is reciprocal. You've probably heard a million times how important communication is in relationships. But do you fully understand exactly what that means? It means that instead of answering a question such as "Is something wrong?" with a sarcastic and emphatic, "NO," you actually tell your sweetheart what the problem is, no matter how embarrassing or difficult it might be. It means remembering that he is not the enemy, but rather, someone who is trying to enhance your life. You see, you are both developing as individuals, and you will continue to do so for the rest of your lives. If you don't keep talking to each other about what those changes are like throughout your lifespan, one day you will wake up and have no idea who that person is sleeping beside you. Development does not stop at puberty; it is a lifelong process, and if you are not open about what is going on in your world all of the time with your significant other, you will at some point literally stop knowing each other. Got it? Communication is so important, it's number one on the Golden Rules list!

The Acceptance Rule

One of the key needs that all of us share is a need for acceptance. As children, we wanted our parents to just love us unconditionally, and accept who we were then. Now, as adults, we would like our achievements, personality traits, and all the general stuff that makes up who we are to be accepted at face value, and not be criticized by others. Thus, there really should be something on your list that reflects this most basic need. For example: "He shouldn't try to change me in any way," or "He should accept the fact that I am _____" (fill in the blank). Are you a huge Rolling Stones fan, a devout Catholic, a strong believer in equal rights? Gay rights? Do you passionately feel that David Hasselhoff should always star in *Jekyll & Hyde* on Broadway? If something is truly, truly important to you as an individual, if it is a belief that will not change unless you decide it should and that may in fact *define* you, then it should be on your list under the heading "acceptance." Remember, this also applies to you accepting him!

The Openness Rule

Keeping it real, being open, and having no expectations (or at least having realistic expectations)—this kind of openness is so important to a healthy relationship. We do know that as we get older we become more open, so my question to you is, why wait? Why take the chance of looking back and saying to yourself, "Darn, he would have been *great* for me, what was I thinking, why did I blow it"? There should be something on your list that shows

···· survey says ····································

Putting information in a list form is really an easy way for researchers to both understand the different traits that happy couples share as well as publicize their findings. Marriage researcher David Fenell found these ten important characteristics that equal marital satisfaction when he studied couples over a twenty-year period in good first marriages.

1. Lifetime commitment to marriage
2. Loyalty to spouse
3. Strong moral values
4. Respect for spouse as a friend
5. Commitment to sexual fidelity
6. Desire to be a good parent
7. Faith in God and/or similar spiritual commitment
8. Desire to please and support spouse
9. Good companion to spouse
10 Willingness to forgive and be forgiven

some forethought and acknowledgment of the big picture. I don't want to see you pass up someone fabulous because you are not as open as you will probably be a few years from now.

Charted Territory

After interviewing hundreds of women for this book, it occurred to me that there was no way I could answer every question that every one of my dear readers had. As the individuals that we are, we find ourselves in so many unique situations that it would be impossible for any book to address them all. However, in the course of my research, I noticed *a lot* of smart, strong women asking me similar questions. Here are a few of the most popular topics we discussed in my interviews, the themes that kept coming up over and over. Really thinking about all of these things will give you insight into how to flesh out some of the items on your list, and will help you make it that much more foolproof.

Jigsaw Boyfriends

Many women who I spoke with when writing this book had said that while they were deciding what they wanted in one man, they had several guys in their lives at once. By dating many men, and not tying yourself down to one guy, you are giving yourself an opportunity to get good perspective on what types of traits really turn you on in a guy. Each guy becomes a separate piece of your puzzle. Much of the time, the guys you are dating all rolled up together would make the perfect guy for you. Think about the qualities you like best in each of the guys you date. Doing that will give you some indication as to whom your future mate should be. The perfect mixture of all the best parts of your exes is out there—trust me.

Are You Too Aggressive?

Have most of your relationships ended because you were ready to take things to the next level and he wasn't? Maybe when he said, "it's not you, it's me," he was wrong! You could be exhibiting aggressive behavior that is sabotaging your success with an otherwise awesome guy.

What is aggression in dating? In women, "aggressive" rarely means violence; it usually means social aggression. What does that look like? It is a range of behaviors aimed at the goal of getting someone to do what you want him to do before he might naturally be ready to do it. Ask yourself, is it after three dates or ten dates that you start to push too much? You can't force someone into a behavior or into feelings: relationships grow at their own pace. You may be feeling some pretty intense feelings for a guy right away, but you have to give yourselves time to let your relationship grow. If you are too aggressive with a man, you may find yourself pushing away a great guy who is just a little gun-shy.

So, you've been told you tend to come on too strong? Usually, socially aggressive women tend to attract men who balance them out. You want someone who can function as the yin to your yang, but you also don't want someone you will have to dominate all the time—it's exhausting. If you can pinpoint the exact time in the relationship when you begin to be a bit pushy, it will speak volumes. Is it when you feel him pull away a bit? Is it when the initial romance begins to wane? Is it when you decide that you like him too, and insecurity has kicked in?

Your "Ex"—The Remix

There are two kinds of "recycled" men. One is the oldie but a goodie from days gone by; the other is a guy who used to go out with one of your friends. If you are bringing back an old flame, there are several guidelines that you need to follow. First of all, ask yourself: Was the time that you dated him long enough in the past? Have you both gone through some drastic changes, meaning that perhaps now he may be datable? Did you finger-paint together in kindergarten, or was he someone you dated briefly in high school and should have taken more seriously? These are situations in which dating him now may be a really good thing, because he is familiar, and you share some history that may connect the two of you in a good way. If he was a guy whom you dated as an adult and you are back with him out of desperation, boredom, frustration, or any other lame reason, then you need to run screaming from that relationship. Dating *anyone* under those circumstances is not a good idea; it makes him the Proximity Guy by proxy.

There are separate rules to follow when the recycled man is your girlfriend's ex. If he is the former lover of someone you no longer socialize with, and you happen to know that he treated her well, then you should feel fine about pursuing him. When analyzing what you know of their past, you must be able to decipher what was his fault, and what was her fault, and you must try to remain objective. Did she date him on the rebound, and is he a nice guy whom she treated badly? Or was she wonderful to him, and he cheated on her? If you find that you have to justify any of his behavior in order to fit him into your paradigm of what a good boyfriend should be, then he is not worth pursuing. And please note: Under *no* circumstances can you date someone who broke a friend's heart if she is still your friend, unless she gives you the go-ahead. Even then, if you value her friendship, proceed with caution.

Retro Dating

Are you making the same dating mistakes you made at sixteen? If you are, you need to sit yourself down and ask yourself, "Why is this not different? Why haven't I changed?" It's fine to make mistakes; everyone does. The key is learning from them. If you don't start learning from your mistakes now, you run the risk of seriously jeopardizing your future happiness. Believe me, the men you are dating have evolved, and you need to do the same. You've got to keep up, girl!

Sex Too Soon?

Recently I was watching an old episode of *The Newlywed Game*, which is a game show from the 1970s featuring four newly married couples who have to answer questions about each other's personality, their likes and dislikes, and so on. If the husband's and wife's answers match up, the couple wins points and eventually a "prize chosen just for them." One question asked during the episode I saw concerned the amount of money the husband spent on the wife, in total, before the first time they "made whoopee" (gotta love the '70s.) Amazingly enough, all four couples had roughly the same answer—about $20, which is equivalent to $100 now—and the reason was because they all had sex on the very

coltrane isn't just a jazz musician, and
collins isn't just a cocktail

In 1991 Scott Coltrane and Randall Collins, two very important sociologists who study marriage and family, asked a group of happily married couples what they considered to be the most significant factors in making a happy marriage. These are the results:

faithfulness was number one, being reported by 93 percent.
understanding was next, with a whopping 86 percent.
a good sex life was agreed upon by 75 percent.
attitudes regarding children garnered 59 percent.
having common interests was reported by 52 percent.

The final three areas were the least endorsed by the study's subjects. Those were:

sharing household chores (43 percent)
having enough money (41 percent)
sharing similar backgrounds (25 percent)

This last item is very interesting because it shows how much can change in just ten to fifteen years. Keep in mind that in 1991 the mean age for marriage was twenty-four for women and twenty-five for men. As of the writing of this book, those ages have risen sharply, to twenty-seven for women and twenty-eight for men. In some urban areas it can be much higher, at thirty-two for both. The research now shows that while all of the other items endorsed by the group cited here may still be extremely valid, the item regarding shared similar backgrounds has had a renaissance.

first date. I then conducted an unscientific poll of my married friends and found that they, too, had not waited very long before "making whoopee," and none waited until they were married. We can't authoritatively say that having sex too soon in a relationship is a mistake of any kind, because there are just too many complexities involved in evaluating sex in a relationship. However, it is not unfair to say that, for some women, having sex too early in a relationship is a bad idea. Being ready to have sex with a person with whom you are entering into a relationship is multifaceted and speaks directly to your personality, your own needs, and the direction that the relationship is taking. The main issue revolves around whether your individual choice to have a sexual relationship with a man has other connotations for you. If you tie sex to expectations that were not previously present between the two of you, or if a sexual connection means an exclusive relationship for you, then you might need to really think about it before you have sex with a new guy. If, on the other hand, sex is just another aspect of getting to know a person for you, one that is not tied to some cosmic, deep, and enduring connection that he now has to live up to, then you can probably feel free to do as you please. You must be very aware of your reasons for having sex in the first place. Since this is book is about breaking patterns, you would be wise to not only figure out relationship patterns, but sexual patterns as well.

Your age is also a factor to consider when deciding if you are ready to have sex with your new guy. Having sex very soon into a relationship at age nineteen has one meaning to a guy and another to the girl, both very specific, especially if you have just begun having sex at all. But having sex very soon into a relationship at age thirty-nine is . . . well . . . really less of a big deal. What you need to be clear about is that it isn't just about sex, unless that is what you are looking for. My main feeling about purely sexual relationships is that they are fine when you are in your twenties and are still trying to figure out your sexual identity, meaning who you are as a sexual being. However, at a certain point, relationships that are purely about sex and devoid of commitment become a waste of your time. Even being in a meaningless sexual relationship while you are searching for Mr. Right can be damaging because, on some level, you are not completely *there*, and you will not be as open to new people as you need to be.

Buyer Beware

All of the questions that you are asking yourself in order to put your perfect Essentials List together are important, but there are a few indicators of more serious problems in previous relationships that you need to be hyper-aware of. Have you been with men in the past who are verbally abusive? Chemically dependent? Clinically depressed? If the answer to any of these questions is "yes," this tendency is something that you need to figure out. This section is going to address the things you might have encountered on your road to finding Mr. Right that are a bit more serious. You should very carefully consider these things, and may even want to seek counseling to address them.

When the Wounded Guy Is Actually the Damaged Guy

If a consistent reason that you have broken up with boyfriends in the past was because "he drank too much," or "he was abusive," or anything that would fit into the category of self-abuse or self-medicating on his part, then it is important to really examine your penchant for dating incredibly damaged guys. Don't try to

go with
what you know

Marriage between two individuals who are, in some culturally important way, similar to each other (race, religion, culture) has been termed *homogamy*, and it is one of the strongest predictors of success in relationships, especially for cohabiting couples. The good news is that the more fundamental similarities you share with Mr. Wonderful, the stronger the likelihood of the two of you being BFF (best friends forever, but in a sexy marriage sort of way). The best research we have is from the couples who have been together the longest. In 1990, Robert and Jeanette Lauer, along with Sarah Kerr, interviewed couples who had been married more than forty-five years. Their study found that couples agreed that the following five items were the most relevant to a long-term marriage:

1. They were married to someone they liked.
2. They had a commitment to the person as well as to the marriage.
3. They had a sense of humor.
4. They were able to reach consensus (agreement) on the more important issues in life.
5. The couples also agreed on goals in life and decision-making, as well as who their friends would be.

explore why they were this way; ask yourself why you've ended up with men who have such serious problems. They were SO damaged, yet you stuck around. Did you have the idea that because you had a terrific family, or are a fabulous person, you could fix them? Have you been through what your exes are going through yourself, and felt that you had a unique understanding that could help? If you have a pattern of falling for guys who are self-destructive, you will need to take a good, hard look at this tendency right now, while you are shaping your list. You might even want to seek professional help, and you most definitely *need* to seek professional help if you are a survivor of a physically or verbally abusive relationship. Obviously, a big list item for you should be to seek out a man who doesn't have these issues, both for your own personal safety and that of the children you may have someday. A self-destructive or abusive man isn't the kind of person you want in your life, and you most certainly do not want someone like this in your children's life, even if he is their father.

It's one thing to go through depression or battle addiction with someone you love, but it is another to be mistreated by someone who just "supposedly" loves you. Dependency of any kind, be it upon drugs, alcohol, gambling, sex, even food, could be just another form of self-medicating. No matter what the dependency is, it is a sign that your guy has something deep and dark that he isn't dealing with. You can't spend your life trying to fix every guy that you meet, especially those who have incredibly destructive, self-medicating behaviors. If this has been your pattern in the past, use this time to figure out what that was about, and how to start anew. You deserve so much better. You deserve to be cherished and loved.

Many women stick it out in relationships with guys like this, and truly believe that if they wait around long enough, "he'll change." Let me tell you this right now: it rarely happens. It's one thing if you are dating a guy who is a little self-destructive, drinks a little too much, passes out, and maybe even makes a fool of himself in public. It's another thing entirely when the abuse is heaped on you. The distinction should be clear, and if the latter sounds familiar to you, you'll need to talk to a professional to find out why you attract these kinds of men. If you honestly can say that he just parties a little too much, then he might just be immature, or masking a deeper problem. In any case, you don't want guys like this. So, "He should not be self-destructive" must be on your list if this has been your pattern.

"Talking a lot" and "Communication": Not the same thing

Communication means more that just wagging your tongue. Take Sally and Marshall, for example. Sally always said that Marshall was a good communicator because he was eager and willing to talk about their problems. However, when they talked, he always seemed to find a way to blame her, someone else, or even his family for whatever issues they were discussing. Marshall was never able to take responsibility for anything that happened in their relationship. This type of talking does not equal communication. Marshall never really opened up to Sally totally; he was never completely vulnerable with her. Although he was always physically talking, he never emotionally connected with anything that Sally said. Looking back on their relationship, Sally jokes that eight years with Marshall felt like eight minutes . . . under water. You can imagine how frustrating it is to be with someone who doesn't shy away from having actual discussions but, when he does talk, also doesn't contribute anything.

Have we sunk so low as women that a man just talking to us about feelings at all is considered communication, no matter what is actually coming out of his mouth? When psychologists refer to "communication" they mean real, honest, from-the-heart, willing-to-be-vulnerable communication. That comes from someone who is not afraid to be judged.

Imaginary Boyfriend

Despite its wild popularity, online dating and e-mail based relationships can actually be a bad idea. Studies of Internet dating explain that, in these types of relationships, the real need for human contact (a.k.a. the reason we date in the first place) is neglected. Furthermore, online dating allows people to develop what researchers call *unrealistic optimism* about the object of their affection. The illusion that you are finding The One and the promise of a relationship is there, but if you are approaching a relationship with unrealistic optimism, that could be cause for clinical concern. For instance, people who are cockeyed optimists, or have invented a person's personality, may distort behavior that should otherwise be seen as negative into something they deem positive. Many people establish serious relationships, and even marry prematurely, based on the illusory belief that they have found "the right one." The only thing online dating should do for you is expand your opportunities by putting you in touch with guys. But you should make a concerted effort to get offline as soon as possible, and foster your new love in the real world.

It's All Fun and Games Until Someone Mentions "Science"

Just telling you what makes a relationship work or why some people stay together for sixty or more years is not enough. You want proof, not opinion about such important matters. And fortunately, so do many, many supremely intelligent and qualified scientific researchers. It may seem like a buzz kill to talk about science, but with the divorce rate as high as it is, you can't go into your new relationship blindly! Offering you some of the research that has been conducted by the aforementioned wise folks of the scientific realm into why some relationships last provides the kind of insight that will help you make the best decisions for yourself when choosing a guy and deciding who is best for you. Then, when you find someone who rocks your world, you will be confident that you can make it an amazing relationship, based on what you know has worked for hundreds of couples before you.

Happily Ever After

Research on happy marriages is important because it gives us a place to start if your Essentials List is shy an item or two. These are the studies you read about that make it seem like there is a secret formula for making relationships work, which only those lucky people who have been in relationships for forty-plus years have figured out. Well, there is a secret formula, and researchers actually have figured out what makes these relationships jibe so well!

When trying to determine the reasons behind a lasting union between two people, relationship satisfaction researchers look at a number of different factors that may lead to marital distress. Some areas that they look at are:

◆ Employment and income of the women
◆ Levels of neuroticism among partners
◆ Premarital cohabitation
◆ Marital status of the couple's parents (i.e., parental divorce)
◆ Religious dissimilarities
◆ History of depression
◆ Age at the time of marriage

These are just some of the aspects of a person's life that have a link to how the person will do in a marriage. It all depends on how well a couple handles things together. Even just one item, such as religious dissimilarities, can be a dealbreaker for some, while others with religious dissimilarities work it out ahead of time. One woman I interviewed was raised by a Jewish father and a Catholic mother. Before her parents had children, they decided that all of the girls would be raised Catholic and the boys raised Jewish. It worked out very well for them. They found a way to adapt to an issue in marriage that could otherwise break up a couple.

When looking at the divorce statistics in this country, it becomes clear that age at the time of marriage is quite pivotal. As of the writing of this book, a 2005 study by the National Center for Health Statistics has revised the divorce rate downward to 43 percent, but that is for the entire nation and thus misleading. If you instead look at the divorce rate for people who marry over the age of thirty and who are educated, the divorce rate is quite low. This means that age at the time of marriage is indeed a factor that can predict marital longevity, as is your level of education. The older you are when you get married, the better your chances of staying married. The same holds true for many of the other items on the list like levels of neuroticism or depression, as well as attitudes about money. These are all factors that, when not discussed ahead of time as to how the couple will handle them, can predict low marital satisfaction and even divorce. You need a plan of action right from the beginning that will help you deal with these factors so that you stay married and don't become another marriage statistic.

Experts Agree

In the early 1990s there was a trend in research to figure out why the divorce rate was so high for some, yet others stayed together thirty, even sixty years. How did they do it? Several researchers set out to find the answers by interviewing thousands of happy couples who have been together forty years or more. They developed all kinds of questionnaires and measurements, such as quizzes. Working with the data they gathered from these interviews and this research, they compiled lists of the Top Ten things that made these happy marriages work, which we will get to shortly. The main point was, if you speak with enough people you start to find consensus about the elements of a good relationship. That way you see that there really are no secrets to a happy marriage; there are only consistent truths that all happy couples share.

Communication Is Key!

Research has shown that communication, as stated before in Cooper's Golden Rules, is one of the pivotal tools that all happy couples have in common. A main theory regarding marriage is that communication strengths and deficits are one of the predictive factors of marriage outcomes. In other words, when we study couples we can tell what the risk that couple has of getting a divorce by how well or how poorly they communicate. Couples with great communication skills are usually good at problem-solving and conflict resolution, another key ingredient for keeping divorce at bay.

The Self-Love Principle

You've got to love yourself first if you want other people to love you back! William Swann, a great thinker in the world of social psychology, had an idea about this concept, which he refers to as "self-verification theory." What that means is that people tend to seek out partners who will verify the way they feel about themselves. So, if your self-esteem is low and you feel bad about who you are, you will seek out the wrong men, just to confirm the crappy ideas you have about yourself. Remember in *Annie Hall*, when Woody Allen quotes the old joke attributed to Groucho Marx, saying, "I would never want to belong to any club that would have someone like me for a member"? Self-verification says that if you think you are a terrible person who doesn't deserve love, then you will seek out people who will not love you. In his studies, Swann showed that depressed people befriended others who saw them in the worst light.

Feeling secure with someone in a relationship and feeling accepted by them can make a difference in your own self-esteem and how you feel about who you are in that relationship. In other words, you need someone who will enhance and encourage those qualities that you know to be your best ones. When you meet someone and you think that he may be special, you need to be mindful of how he sees you. We have all been in that situation, where you say one thing and the person totally misconstrues what you've said, and no matter how many times we try to explain ourselves, the person is just not getting it. It's almost like trying to explain to your grandmother what a blog is before she even understands the Internet—it's just frustrating. This illustrates the type of situation to avoid. What you want is someone you are completely simpatico with; you want someone who totally gets you.

When we are with people who get us, then there is potential for self-enhancement, and it becomes more difficult to focus on the worst in yourself, as so many self-critical women are apt to do. This is a very important point for you to get because if you can bond with a guy you are interested in (even a small amount) then you have potential there. In other words, if you see that the person understands you on some level, that you've made a real connection, then as far as your self-esteem goes, potential equals positive. It can be as meaningful as sharing a common upbringing or as innocuous as a favorite ice-cream flavor. Some research has shown that when women share a birthday with an attractive person (male or female), it can actually enhance their self-esteem. Go figure.

chapter thirteen

been there, done that, got the ring anyway

So, you've asked all the right questions, compiled all the answers, and even foolproofed your list using proven scientific theory! All of this evaluating and planning has really put you in good shape to get out there and find your Mr. Right. But where does the romance fit into all of this? We didn't lose it in the course of all that planning, did we? Of course not!

This chapter is going to be about Essentials List success stories. These are the stories of real-life women who've *Been There, Done That*, gotten the ring, and tied the knot! They will be the first to tell you that no matter how much planning you do, finding Mr. Right is never going to be completely formulaic. It did help them, though, to have a plan in their heads so that when there was some correlation between what they were looking for and what they found, they pounced instead of ran.

Here are their stories.

Susie and Jonathan's Story

Susie says, "I dated *a lot.* No exaggeration—I probably went on 250 dates in my single life before meeting Jonathan. I had three very serious relationships, each lasting about two years. The one previous to Jonathan was a major catch. He was a very wealthy day trader. On paper he was the dream man, a good-looking hunk; he was the Bachelor, the guy you show off to everyone and it was like, 'ha, I got him.' I managed to hold on to him for three years, but it was turmoil all the time. We had amazing physical chemistry, but some aspects of the relationship made me feel terrible all the time. The highs were really high and the lows were so low that it never felt right. Unfortunately, he was also a little bit of a Proximity Guy (he lived in the adjoining building), so when we finally broke up, I found out he was dating someone else because I saw them together—the very next day.

"When I moved out of that building, I moved to the Upper West Side of Manhattan, where I think I dated everyone remotely attractive. I was the girl who didn't say no; I was totally up for anything and after a few years, I think I exhausted my options. This one night I went with my friends to one of those synagogue singles nights, even though I didn't really date Jewish guys and it was not my scene. I didn't think I would meet anyone there, and kind of thought it was a waste of time, but then I saw a great-looking guy across the crowded room. I turned to my friend and said, 'Do you know that guy? I have to go out with him!' One guy who knew him wouldn't introduce us because he said I would only break his heart, but I kept asking around the party until I found someone who knew him, and he introduced us. He said to Jonathan: 'See that girl over there? She wants to go out with you!'"

Now, a little background about Susie: Susie always liked Younger Guys and usually dated them, but it never worked out, because there was always too much of an age difference. So, when Susie found out that Jonathan was only four years younger than she was, she knew that this was a step in the right direction. (But just in case, she lied about her age.) Anyway, Jonathan called the next night, and on the phone, she realized that he had an accent. After the phone call, Jonathan had two strikes against him. One was that she had a hard time understanding him over the phone because of his accent, and the second was that, now that he was interested in her, she just didn't like him as much.

Nevertheless, she went out on a date with Jonathan. The place was loud, and don't forget the accent, so between the two, Susie couldn't understand a word that Jonathan was saying. Because she had no idea what he was talking about, she found herself laughing throughout the entire date. Jonathan thought that they were having a great date because she was laughing the whole time, but in reality, Susie was laughing because she thought it hilarious that she didn't understand anything he said!

Susie had made a rule for herself to go on three dates before dumping a guy. For date number two, he took her to the Metropolitan Opera. Jonathan knew that Susie liked opera, so taking her there in the first place definitely earned him brownie points. In the middle of the opera, during intermission, Jonathan wanted to leave. Her immediate thought was: "Hmmm, I love the opera, he wants to leave, not a good sign." However, Susie was pretty adamant about her three-date rule, so she decided to give him one more shot before she conveniently lost his number.

The day that they chose for the third date was Susie's birthday and, having lied to him about her age in the first place, she didn't really want him to know which birthday it was. So, Susie invited Jonathan out after her birthday celebration. It was an unremarkable evening, and they weren't meshing at all.

"So," Susie recalls, "I figured that was it. The next day I went snowboarding with my friends and I wasn't very good at it, and believe it or not I broke both wrists! I was rushed to the emergency room and by the time the day was done, I had both arms in casts. I was totally depressed, so my friend took me out to lunch. Now keep in mind that with both arms in casts, it is nearly impossible to blow-dry your hair, and forget about the intricacies of putting on makeup. I looked my worst! So, we walked into the restaurant, which was a kind of cafeteria, and of course there was Jonathan. He got up and walked away and I said to my friend, 'If he had come over here or done something to help I might have said that he was the kind of guy you marry!' Then, suddenly he appeared with a drink in his hand . . . for me! He had walked away to get me a tray and a drink because he saw that I couldn't use my arms. I looked at him in a whole different light. We were engaged shortly after that, after the moment when I saw what kind of person he was. I really saw him in that one moment, and I'm glad that I gave him the chance that I almost didn't."

And the Moral of the Story Is . . .

Your prince charming might not always make the best first impression, whether the reason be nerves or lack of experience in dating you. So try to keep your mind open with the guys you meet, because they may reveal their true selves to you in seemingly innocuous ways. If you aren't paying attention, you might miss them. Just think about it: All of the reasons that Susie was turned off by Jonathan—his accent, his desire to leave the opera early—were silly, self-involved little details. If she hadn't been paying attention, she very well may have missed the boat with her Mr. Right!

Philomena and Gregory's Story

Before Gregory, who was her Mr. Right, Philomena was in several long-term romances. Much of the time during those relationships, she and the guy she was with discussed a future together, because that's just what you did. It wasn't like she really had those feelings, necessarily; it was more like, "We've been together two years, now what?" By the time Philomena met Gregory, she felt ready to commit to someone for the rest of her life, to find The One, because she had already dated most of the *Been There, Done That* guys. She dated some of them for six months, some of them for three, and some of them for even less time, but for the most part, she had been at a point in her life where she was determined to go through as many of them as she could muster up the energy for.

Philomena says, "My dating pattern before I met Gregory was very systematic, meaning 'let me check off all of these types from my list and get it out of my system.'" The Older Guy was first; he came complete with a job and a mustache, her only two criteria at the time besides wanting to date someone who was "much older." She met the Party Guy at a fraternity party (where else?), and they had fun getting drunketty-drunk-drunk and skipping classes together. The Workout Guy was a professional athlete. Every girl gets to date at least one high-profile guy in her life and this was hers, and it was at a time when her best friend was dating the local weatherman on Channel 4, so it seemed only fair. She met the Hot Guy at her speech and communication class at a local community college. He gave a speech about a nearby restaurant, and while going over their menu he included "quickie" as an item. She approached him after class to ask what a quickie was; he showed her the menu, which said ham and cheese quiche. To this day when she bakes a quiche at home, she refers to it as a quickie, a homage to his sheer beauty and downright stupidity. Finally, Philomena dated her version of the Wounded Guy, who was also Proximity Guy (two disasters in one). He was a man in her office who lived across the street from her *and* had just lost his mother. She slept with him for pity's sake, and roll call was completed.

Philomena concludes: "I realized that despite their stereotypes, who they were at their core was what counted. And at their very cores, all of those guys were too damaged to take seriously."

Philomena and Gregory met in 2002, when both were living in Massachusetts. He was in the Navy and she was working at a horse farm while living with her boyfriend of three years. Philomena said that with Gregory it was love at first sight. She knew that she was with the wrong guy the minute she saw Gregory, even though she didn't really know him yet. She decided to take the risk and break up with her long-term boyfriend to take a cross-country trip with Gregory the summer before he had to return to the Navy. When she smashed his car somewhere near California, Gregory took it in stride. He simply rented another one, and said: "I said I would show you the Pacific Ocean and by gosh, I'm going to." His determination—and lack of desire to absolutely kill her for totaling his car—showed her his character right away. She saw that he was unfazed by material things, one of the characteristics that she loves about him to this day. Philomena says, "We took a train back to the East Coast and he went back to the Navy, while I went back to college. We decided that since it was long distance, we should date other people—but neither of us did. Every guy that I met, I compared to Gregory, and they paled in comparison, so I knew that I should wait. Even though I was older, I thought the risk of waiting versus being alone was a fair one."

And the Moral of the Story Is . . .

When you meet your Mr. Right, you might know immediately. Like Philomena, many women find themselves in situations where they are settling for less than they truly want in a relationship, and end up discussing a future or even marrying or starting a family with the wrong guy because it "seems like the right thing to do." Just because settling down with someone seems like the next logical step, it doesn't always mean that you've found your true love. It doesn't matter what your family thinks, or that your friends are all settling down. Those are their lives, not yours. You need to listen to your heart when you're out there in the dating world, and you need to never stop listening to it, even after you've found someone you think is great. If you want to be truly happy, you must always keep a close eye on your own heart, and be constantly in touch with what you want out of life, and what you need from your life partner. Philomena broke up with a long-term boyfriend on what probably seemed to her friends and family like a ridiculous whim, but it wasn't; it was likely the best decision she's ever made. Don't be afraid to take risks like that when you know it's right. Learn to trust yourself. The most perfect guy for you is out there, I promise, and he just might blindside you by showing up in your life at a seemingly inopportune time. Darn that love and its timing!

Grace and Tom's Story

Grace says, "I have to admit that I was always lucky in love. I never dated guys who I ever referred to in any negative way and I always had great boyfriends. My love life was off to a great start right from the very beginning. My first boyfriend in high school, my first love, was an incredible first love. It was the kind of relationship that you usually have in your forties. It was trusting, open, and honest; he was my best friend. We dated for four years, and I have to say that he set the bar pretty high, so I always knew that was what I wanted from a boyfriend, and I always looked for that kind of relationship. Some of my relationships had it, some of them didn't. I was madly in love three times.

"Then I dated around for a bit, and it was during a time when I was looking for the wrong things. I dated the Hot Guy, who was also a singer. He was very intelligent (a rarity when it comes to the Hot Guy archetype) as well as pompous, which was very daring for a guy living on a friend's couch. Oh, did I mention he was also a lot younger? But I was nuts for him.

"My last boyfriend before I met Tom didn't work, mostly because we wanted totally different things, but more so because we were similar in the wrong ways. His name was Cary, like Cary Grant, and he was an actor. We were born a day apart, both fire signs, both in the arts, and both highly competitive people, and it was drama all the time. What I learned from him was not to mistake drama for passion and emotion. We would cry hard and fight hard and love hard and have these dramatic ups and downs and I realized after we broke up that you can be passionate and be on an even keel: it doesn't have to be a knock-down, drag-out fight for there to be passion in a relationship. I made sure to look for that in my next relationship. It was at the top of my Essentials List. I mistook 'unstable' for 'passion,' so while it sounds like it should have been obvious, mental stability was my Essential number two.

"With Tom, when we have a problem we talk about it and then move on. We don't need to get to that state of high drama to be passionate about each other. As a matter of fact, it is the lack of drama that makes our relationship more passionate, because we can communicate and are so close. I never realized that communication could be such an aphrodisiac.

"In the end I realized that Tom was all of my exes rolled into one: he was the best of the worst, and the best of the best at the same time. All of the best qualities that I loved in each of my *Been There, Done That* guys, I found in Tom. I don't know if I can say it was love at first sight, but I do remember that when I first met him, I told a friend, 'He's the kind of guy I could marry.'

"We actually met at a wedding, but it was really less of a wedding and more of a weeklong extravaganza. We were both in this twenty-two-person wedding party accompanied by about seventy friends who were invited to the endless wedding events. Actually, now that I think about it, the odds were with us that someone would be single, since half of Rhode Island was there. With all there was to do and all of the food (and there was tons) at every event, I started running on the beach just to keep up. One morning Tom saw me after my run and asked if we could meet up to run together the next day.

"From that first run there were never any games; we made a very honest connection early on. The only problem was that he lived in another city, so if we were going to do the long-distance thing it had to be worth it. Every single weekend we saw each other and it was great because I was single all week, then had him on the weekends. After about a year we wanted to be in the same city, but who would go where? He immediately began looking for jobs in my city, and we agreed that if I got the one and only job I wanted that would make me move, we would live in his city. Sure enough, I got that job."

And the Moral of the Story Is . . .

The most important moral to Grace's story is to save the drama for the movies—it doesn't work in real life. It only adds stress to your everyday existence that will eat away at you, and erode your self-esteem as time goes on. That kind of weird passion, or really instability in this case, just isn't cute after twenty-five. Think of your dating past as "research." Sure, you may have a bunch of failed relationships under your belt, but only after dating all of these duds can you figure out what you really want from a guy. Unfortunately, good decision-making comes from making bad decisions. It all depends on your learning curve.

Angie and Gene's Story

There are two things that Angie always knew about herself. One was that she wanted to make films, and the other was that she was never very into dating. She never felt comfortable being on a "date" with a total stranger, so when she started dating her first serious boyfriend, which was when she was very young, she just kept the relationship going. This explains why Angie ended up stuck in a rut with that rare and dreadful Wounded Guy / Clingy Guy combo. It was the bipolar dating coup of a lifetime and a true test of wills, hers against his, on a daily basis. Since this was her first real relationship, she didn't know that wasn't how things were supposed to go. He went back and forth from being the Wounded Guy to being the Clingy Guy from one day to the next, and she never quite knew which one she was getting on which day. On Tuesday he was obsessively overprotective, and then by Wednesday he was really, really sorry and vulnerable and loving—until Friday rolled around, when he was needy again and suspicious of anyone and anything that could have taken her away from him, and even yelled at her when the bank teller took a little extra time with her deposit.

Angie spent her days wondering, "What is he going to think if I do this or that?" She put up with it for several years because she was afraid to end it out of both loyalty and fear that he would disintegrate if she left him.

Finally, he just beat the love out of her emotionally. She got up the nerve to dump him. Then she moved, changed her phone number, her job, and even contemplated changing her name, but couldn't come up with anything that sounded as cute as "Angie."

After she broke up with the Wounded Guy/Clingy Guy, Angie dated and hated. That's when you date because you think you should, but you dread every minute of it and every aspect of it. This is the "what do I wear, what do I say, what if he doesn't like me" syndrome, which includes every other possible question that you can ask yourself to make the experience as unpleasant as possible. It was all too much for her. It stands to reason, then, that when she went in for the interview at a sound studio and saw this foxy sound engineer named Rex, she was relieved. Aside from thinking, "I could totally work here!" she also thought she could finally just take her time and get to know this guy and not have to do any of that dating craziness that she hated so much. He came on really strong, which she mistook for intense interest.

Rex was charming, but it was more like a verb than an adjective, something he was doing to her: he charmed her; he was The Bachelor. And since he was such a hottie, Angie did not proceed with caution and maintain speed, but rather followed his lead full force. She didn't have a lot of dating experience and had certainly never seen the likes of The Bachelor before. True to form, after two months he was bored, lost interest, and stopped being attentive to her. Heartbroken and totally rejected, with her confidence in the toilet, Angie trudged on. After all, she still had to work with him! Angie tried to maintain a friendship with Rex until the day when he asked about a friend of hers who came into the office, who he thought was cute. This was more than she could take.

During her bedlam with The Bachelor, Angie confided in another coworker, named Gene. She told Gene about Rex and how hurt she was the day she answered the phone at work and it was his new girl on the other line (who he did the same thing to, as it turned out: hot, heavy, over.) She told Gene she thought it had been a huge mistake to date a coworker, and how sorry she was that she ever did that.

Now, Gene had a girlfriend in another state at the time, and agreed that sometimes too close for comfort is exactly that: too close! Angie said that she and Gene always had a friendship that was "first-grade flirty," where the guy picks on you because he likes you, but she thought that in this case it was harmless, because they were both in other relationships. She never thought of Gene "like that." Gene would tease her by leaving messages about her on sound equipment around the office, making fun of her in a cute way, like about what she was wearing that day or how she smelled. It was a running joke between them.

Angie said that the day she realized he might like her more than just a flirty office thing went like this: "He had left a broom in my office with a note that said 'saw this in the hallway . . . was wondering how you got home.'" Angie said that this quirky relationship inspired her to make a short film, one that did very well and got her back into filmmaking. She said that Gene, on some level, was like a muse. Since he was in a relationship she, of course, thought nothing more of it, and never thought anything would ever happen with them. Gene worked nights and was home the morning of September 11 while Angie was in the office, a few blocks north of the twin towers. Angie's phone rang.

"I was in the city, and he called to see if I was okay. On *that* day, he thought of me. We talked for a while and he said 'maybe you should get out of the city' and I thought that maybe I should because it was just too upsetting and chaotic, besides which, the next day was also my birthday. I still refused to believe that anything was going to happen; we worked together and he had a girlfriend. Then on my birthday he showed up with a huge box; a DVD player, which was a hilarious gift since he liked to tease me that I was completely behind technology-wise, which I really was. I asked him about his girlfriend and he kept avoiding the conversation. I think he didn't want to come on too strong and he had heard that I was dating this other guy, which wasn't true. We talked until four o'clock in the morning. My friends all told me to move on because he was never going to leave this girl. Well, I had to know, I was really interested in him at this point, but I did not want to get clobbered yet again. I called him up and asked him to come over. I was ready to give back the DVD, change jobs, whatever I had to do, it was just all too much. Living in the city at this particular time plus all of this emotional relationship stuff . . . I was burned out! I really wanted to be in relationship again and I couldn't be friends with Gene knowing he was with someone else, it was just too painful. So, I invited him over and told him that I had to give him back his gift, and said 'I can't do this.' He looked at me and said, 'I broke up with my girlfriend weeks ago! I've been trying to tell you, but I didn't think you were done with Rex, and I thought that you wouldn't go out with me because we worked together.'

"Then he said, 'I think we would be really amazing together and this could be something really special if you were willing to give it a chance.'" Angie said that she broke down right there and he held her until she fell asleep. Angie remembers, "When I woke up I realized that he was right. This friendship was the best thing that ever happened to me and since I never started like that with anyone before, I didn't realize how great it could be. We connected so well and I learned that it could be a good prescription for a relationship." Turns out, Gene was right; it worked out, and Angie and Gene just bought their first house together. Angie says, "I would say it worked out very nicely, and I never looked back."

And the Moral of the Story Is . . .

Beware if your concept of true love is that it's something that happens at first sight. Some women, especially those who have a lousy track record with guys, that philosophy has not served them well. Instead they become clouded by hot lusty feelings, interpret attraction for the real thing, and wind up brokenhearted because they've been putting all of their energy into dating the wrong guy. Some people are also just "beginning of relationship" junkies: they like the hot attraction, and then when the bloom is off the rose, they move on. It's a very immature way to live and if you persist in this behavior as you get older, it actually becomes quite tragic. Sometimes doing something different, like dating someone you already know, or someone who you wouldn't normally look twice at, might be just the elixir you have been looking for. Angie and Gene's relationship is also a testimony to the research you previously read, a real-life example of how good communication, respect, and a solid friendship are the real cornerstones to a long-lasting relationship. When you are truly ready to have a mature, adult relationship, you will start to behave differently, and ask for more from a potential Mr. Right. You will no longer be willing to settle, and when you find that right guy for you, you'll suddenly realize that being adored and respected is totally where it's at.

conclusion

You can make the wrong choices over and over, but all it takes is one right choice to be with the man of your dreams, and trust me, he is just around the corner. You are a wonderful, capable woman who *will* find her perfect match. It is impossible that you will end up alone, as long as you get to know yourself first and figure out what is best for you in your future. There are many ways to go about discovering who you are and what you want, and by articulating your Essentials List, you are off to an excellent start especially if what you want is love. You will be happy, as long as happiness is your one true goal, and you are realistic and honest about what you need to achieve it. When you learn that life is about who you have loved and who has loved you back, you will have a better chance at real happiness. It is imperative that you measure the men you date by the size of their hearts, and not the size of their wallets.

If all else fails, remember these three jewels of advice, which my grandmother gave me and I am now giving to you. Every woman should follow them. She said:

1. When he takes you out on a date, let him pay.
2. Marry a man who loves you more than you love him.
3. Always wear lipstick.

references

Brown, J. D., Novick, N. J., Lord, K. A., & Richards, J. M. (1992). When Gulliver travels: Social context, psychological closeness, and self-appraisals. *Journal of Personality and Social Psychology,* 62, 717–727.

Coltrane, S., & Collins, R. (2000). *Sociology of Marriage and the Family: Gender, Love, and Property* (5th edition). Florence, KY: Wadsworth Publishing.

Fenell, D. L. (1993). Characteristics of long-term first marriages. *Journal of Mental Health Counseling,* 15, 446–460.

Knobloch, L. K., & Solomon, D. H. (2003). Manifestations of relationship conceptualizations in conversation. *Human Communication Research,* 29, 482–515.

Lauer, R. H., *Lauer,* J. C., & *Kerr,* S. T. (1990). The long-term marriage: Perceptions of stability and satisfaction. *International Journal of Aging & Human Development,* 31, 189–195.

Loevinger, J., & Wessler, R. (1970). *Measuring Ego Development.* San Francisco: Jossey-Bass.

Lutwak, N. (1985). Fear of intimacy among college women. *Adolescence*, 20, 15–20.

Murray, S. L., Rose, P., Holmes, J. G., Derrick, J., Podchaski, E. J., Bellavia, G., et al. (2005). Putting the partner within reach: A dyadic perspective on felt security in close relationships. *Journal of Personality and Social Psychology*, 88. 327-347.

Robinson, L. C., & Blanton, P. W. (1993). Family relations: Marital strengths in enduring marriages. *Interdisciplinary Journal of Applied Family Studies*, 42, 38–45.

Stanley, S. M., Markman, H. J., & St. Peters, M. (1995). Strengthening marriages and preventing divorce: Family relations. *Journal of Applied Family & Child Studies*, 44, 392–401.

Yuan, N. P. (2003). How does yesterday affect our relationship today? Intraindividual variability in satisfaction, positive affect, and interaction behaviors among dating couples. *Dissertation Abstracts International: Section B: The Sciences & Engineering*, 63, 10B. pp. 4932.

Swann, W. B., Hixon, J. G., & De La Ronde, C. (1992). Embracing the bitter "truth": Negative self-concepts and marital commitment. *Psychological Science*, 3, 118–121.

about the author

As a radio host, developmental psychologist, and, quite frankly, as a woman, Cooper Lawrence's favorite topic is dating . . . but not *just* dating; rather, endless discussion about The One. When will I meet him? Is he the guy I'm dating now? Is he really out there? How do I know I didn't flip him off on the subway? On her radio show and in real life, Cooper can talk for hours and hours about the subject, answering questions from callers and friends alike, and in doing so she has found a formula that will help you actually answer the question . . . Is he The One? When put together, the *Been There, Done That, Kept the Jewelry* guys and their antidote, the Essentials List, are the perfect formula for answering that age-old question, and it has proven to be successful time and time again.

A classic overachiever, Cooper has dated all the *Been There, Done That, Kept the Jewelry* guys, and through the wreckage has found her magnificent man muffin, whom she married in April 2005.

Raised in New York, Cooper began her career at the alternative radio station WLIR after some success in the world of voice-overs. Since then Cooper has worked and continues to work in New York as a regular swing at Z100, KTU, and Q104.3 radio.

Her part-time working status allowed her to attend Fordham University, first for her master's, which she received in 2002, and then for her doctorate in psychology on a presidential scholarship. During her first year at Fordham University, Cooper worked morning radio shifts, attended school during the day, and produced *The Joan Rivers Show* from 6 to 8 P.M. for WOR.

True to her overachieving personality, Cooper not only has a degree in psychology, but also has published dozens of articles in *CosmoGIRL!* magazine, *Mode* magazine, *Backstage*, and many more. Her first book, *A Guide to Guys* (Sterling Publications), has sold out on Amazon.com and BarnesandNoble.com, and has been translated into several languages.

Currently . . .

Magazines: As an advisory board member of *CosmoGIRL!* magazine, Cooper helps to shape the direction of the magazine and is especially proud being "The Love Doctor." Yet another opportunity to spin her psychological magic.

Radio: Cooper has her own FM Real Talk for Women radio show on 107.9 THE LINK in Charlotte, NC (Monday through Friday, 7 P.M.-10 P.M.) simply called "The Cooper Lawrence Show" where she will lovingly discuss any and all relationship issues, and anything else on your mind, with callers from around the country. You can listen live online at *www.1079thelink.com*.

Television: Cooper hosts a new show for The Discovery Channel. The show looks at some old sociological standbys to see if they are alive and well or if they have gone the way of the dinosaur. Are people still obedient to authority in 2006? Are they willing to comply with a big request after complying with a smaller one? The science says yes; to see what the public does, go to *www.discovery.com* for show times in your area.

And in New York, Cooper can also be seen regularly as an expert on WPIX New York's WB11 *Morning News*.